THOMAS PENDLEBURY – A Lanc

Bryan Hughes was born in Atherton, Lancashire, in 1932, where he attended the old Hesketh Fletcher Senior School, later going to Leigh Technical College and Wigan & District Mining & Technical College.

As a young chorister at Howe Bridge Parish Church he became interested in the organ, its music, construction and history.

He regularly writes on this subject and has given a number of invited lectures at various universities to architectural students. He has been responsible for the restoration and the building of a number of pipe organs, and specialises in the study of the work of the famous 19th century European organbuilder Edmund Schulze. He is also responsible for organising choral, orchestral and organ concerts, and has worked in this field with local radio and BBC Radio 3. A past President of the Wigan & District Organists' Association and a member of various associations including the Incorporated Association of Organists; The British Institute of Organ Studies: The Victorian Society. Bryan was a Local Government Officer before retiring in 1993.

With Every Good Wish

Bryan Hughes

Thomas Pendlebury (1867-1933)

THOMAS PENDLEBURY

A Lancashire Craftsman

by
Bryan Hughes

OWL
BOOKS

First published October 1993 by
Owl Books
P.O. Box 60
Wigan WN1 2QB

ISBN 1 873888 55 4

Designed, typeset and produced by Coveropen Ltd., Wigan.

Text produced via high resolution DTP Garamond Cond. 11/12.5pt

Printed and bound in Great Britain by Redwood Books, Trowbridge, Wiltshire

CONTENTS

To Eileen
for an abundance of help, patience and understanding.

ACKNOWLEDGEMENTS

The author's grateful thanks are due to the following people, libraries etc., who have so willingly offered their help and shared their memories: James Pendlebury, Edward Collier, the late Cyril Ward, Henry Ashcroft M.A., Sheila Woodward, Harry Manifold (Organist Leigh Baptist Church). Dorothy Wilson, Richard Coates, Revd. Father Collingwood P.P. Sacred Heart Catholic Church, Leigh. William Rigby, Thomas Fell, Revd. Father Gamble P.P. St. Joseph's Catholic Church, Leigh. William N. Blakey, Maurice Maloney (Organist St. Joseph's Catholic Church, Leigh). Nora Welsby, Frank Winstanley, Lily Edwards, the late Stanley Pendlebury F.I.O.B. (Managing Director The Pendlebury Organ Company). Alfred Hayes (Manager, New Mill Bedford Square, Leigh). Roger Marsh, Evelyn S. Finch (Chairman Liverpool & S.W. Lancashire Family History Society). The staff of Leigh Library and The Central Library, Manchester. The late Percy & George S. Johnson, Charles A. Myers L.R.A.M., A.R.C.O., L.G.S.M. (Hons) L.T.C.L., Arthur Scholes, Revd. Father Dr. L.R. Wells Ph.L., S.T.L., P.P. St. Cuthbert's Catholic Church, Blackpool. The staff of the *Leigh Reporter* and the *Leigh Journal*, the late Roy Taylor F.T.C.L., L.R.A.M., (Organist of St. Andrew's Church, Wigan). The Revd. Hargreaves-Stead L.Th., Vicar of St. Paul's Parish Church, Westleigh. The invaluable help of Nicholas Webb M.A., Len Hudson and Ann Baxter (staff of Wigan Record Office). Finally to Eileen R. Leedam whose help as proof reader was invaluable and to Betty Pendlebury for the loan of material and photographs and without whose help and co-operation this work could not have been written.

PREFACE

This is the story of a Lancashire craftsman and his sons. Possessed with a natural gift and an inbuilt sensitivity, Thomas Pendlebury struggled from humble circumstances during the closing years of the 19th century to become a famous organ builder in his native town of Leigh, Lancashire. His fame quickly spread throughout Yorkshire, Cumbria and eventually the U.S.A.

Fortunately many examples of his art still survive. One trusts they will be preserved as part of our musical heritage.

CHAPTER 1

Early History of Westleigh

ARLY records reveal that the Manor of Westleigh was constituted in the 12th century under the ownership of the Botelers of Warrington; later this ownership was passed to Roger, Lord of Marsey in Nottinghamshire. By the mid-1200s Roger of Marsey had sold his Lancashire fee, which included the Manor of Westleigh, to the Earl of Chester. Eventually it passed into the Duchy of Lancashire.

The head of one of the oldest families of the Manor of Westleigh was Geoffrey de Westleigh in the reign of Richard I. It is thought that he built a church there in the latter part of the 12th century. Sometime in the year 1200 A.D. there was a certain John de Westleigh holding a title of 'Parson of Westleigh', and was in – or having possession of, the right to appoint an incumbent to the living in the church of Westleigh. John de Westleigh had three sons, Richard, Adam and Alan. Of these, Richard succeeded to the manor of Kirk Hall. Later when a decree was issued ordering that every church should have a properly ordained clergy entitled to a glebe (a piece of land for his support), Richard de Westleigh vacated the church premises and built a large house which he named Higher Hall.

Richard de Westleigh died without issue, and was succeeded by his brother, Adam. Before his death Richard had presented half the church with the right of presentation of the living to the Priory of Wallingford. This is recorded in 1233 by an assize court to determine the ownership of the said church – either Adam de Westleigh or the Prioress of Wallingford. It appears that the verdict went in favour of the Prioress, for it was she who appointed the successive incumbent.

Adam de Westleigh married Quenhilda, by whom he had a son, Roger, the last of the male line to hold the Manor of Westleigh. Roger married Emma de Shoreworth, they had one daughter, Sigreda, she later married Richard de Urmston of Flixton. Richard purchased the right to appoint incumbents to the Manor of Westleigh from the Prioress of Wallingford in 1292; and the Manor stayed in their ownership throughout the years of the Commonwealth.

The Urmston family was staunch Catholic, and in those days of religious intolerance and the fears generated by 'Gun Powder Plot', adherents of the 'old faith' were subject on the least provocation to fines and imprisonment and the confiscation of their lands. Under the 1641 act of Protestation 'to obtain and defend the true reformed Protestant Religion against all Popery & Popish innovations'. The Urmston's suffered these penalties, and although Richard had taken no part in the Civil War no doubt his sympathies were with the Royalists. For this he was arrested as an enemy of the state, along with his son-in-law Richard Shuttleworth and several others. There were eighteen known Catholic residents at this time in Westleigh. The estates and lands were taken over by the Commissioner of Forfeited Estates and sold in sections of fourth parts, to the Atherton family of Atherton; the Hiltons of Pennington Hall; John and William Hall of Walmersely, Bury. Thus the old manorship of Westleigh passed away forever, in this way many estates passed from England's oldest families.

LEIGH AND WESTLEIGH IN THE NINETEENTH CENTURY

BY 1857 the importance of the coal industry led to the formation of a Coal Miners Association, which met monthly at the George & Dragon, Leigh. The following collieries were represented – Astley & Bedford; Springfield; Hayfield; Broadfield; James Diggles and Westleigh. Apart from this industry, spinning was carried out on simple spinning wheels and on hand-looms by cottagers and small farmers. The agriculture worked on these small farms around Leigh and Westleigh was of a very simple kind, the heavier tasks being undertaken by the male members of the family, whilst the farmer's wife and daughters attended to the churning, cheese-making and household tasks. When this work was done the family spent any spare time in spinning cotton or wool. A farmer would have three or four looms in his house, and if he could pay the rent on his smallholding by the profits from this kind of work, then so much the better. Cottage rents in the late 1800s would be from one-and-a-half to two guineas per year. And a man's wage was from eight to ten shillings per week.

In 1863 the Local Government Act came into existence, where each District was under the jurisdiction of its own elected board. But with the close proximity of these districts, it was proposed in 1874 that an Urban District Council of Leigh should be formed and divided into wards viz Westleigh, Pennington, Bedford and part of Atherton. The amalgamation order was completed on June 14th 1875 by the Local Government Board and the beginning of the Leigh Borough was founded.

CHAPTER 2

The Pendleburys of Lancashire

EARLY YEARS

THE closing years of the 19th century was a period which saw the development of the modern organ as we know it today. Indeed, the whole of the century was abundant with inventors and idealists, who believed in their craft and art. Amongst these was one Thomas Pendlebury, who began life as a 'pit boy' working in the mines, became an inventor, and finally an organbuilder who was eventually accepted by the famous leading organbuilders of his time.

Thomas Pendlebury was born in 1867 on a smallholding between Dangerous Corner and St. Paul's Church, Westleigh, Lancashire; an area known locally as 'Top o'th Bottoms'. He was the first child of eight children born to Robert Pendlebury and his wife Ellen, who scratched a living out of the soil of Westleigh. The 'Rate Books' for 1890 record the Pendlebury smallholding at 206 Westleigh Lane, with a yearly rate of £1-6s-8d. The property was rented from John Green, Walmsley Road, Leigh who owned several other properties in Westleigh

Robert Pendlebury (Farmer), aged 93. Born circa 1822.

Lane. In 1867 Westleigh was a poor unfashionable area, the least desirable for a residence. The land was pockmarked with both drift and shaft mines, and with the spoil heaps of their workings. Hardly a likely cradle for someone whose name was eventually to be revered and respected by those in the refined atmosphere of the organ loft.

The Pendleburys' were a respected family locally, both resourceful and hard working; and, so we are told, 'of sober habits'. Tom's father, Robert, had not allowed the difficulties of those times to hang heavily upon him. He encouraged his children to have interests other than those of mere survival.

The children of Robert and Ellen Pendlebury were:

Thomas – became the renowned Lancashire organbuilder.

James – worked in the mines. In order to study mining at Wigan & District Mining & Technical College, he would walk from Westleigh to Wigan and back in the evenings, a distance of some ten miles. In his final year he won a Gold Prize Medal. James later became colliery manager at Swan Lane Colliery, Hindley Green.

Joseph – served in the Great War 1914-18. At one period was coachman at Westleigh Hall. Later lived at Little Lever, Bolton as a farmer.

Robert – little information.

Roger – killed in a mine accident at the age of 16.

Emma – no information.

Mary – known as Polly to the family.

Helen – youngest daughter, kept house for Robert her father.

Thomas had left school by the time he was eight years old. He helped his father on the small farm, and by today's standards was uneducated. An incident Thomas recalls clearly was when walking with his mother past Leigh Parish Church. He asked, 'What is the noise?' Being told that it was a 'large bell', he then asked 'how many bells were ringing?' as apparently he could hear the harmonics so distinctly and assumed that a number of bells were ringing.

In 1879 when he was eleven years old young Tom Pendlebury was working in the mine at Eatock Pit, Hindley. It was at this time, young though he was, that Thomas' parents discovered that he might possibly have a 'musical ear'. In fact he was later found to possess what is known as 'perfect pitch'. Tom could pick out the harmonics of bells quite distinct from their ground tone. It is said that he would cry out as if in pain at sounds which were discordant, although perhaps this was not so unusual from a member of a family whilst respected locally, were never-the-less regarded as a bit eccentric.

At this stage in his life the family did not possess any musical instrument. But when he was about thirteen years old Thomas was allowed into the parlour of a friend's house and there saw an old table piano with yellow keys. He assumed that the sound from this instrument was created by hammers striking wires. He then attempted to make something similar, but with little progress for when he did manage to get a hammer to strike a wire, there was no tone. A soundboard was required as he was to discover some years later when he came across the carcase of an old upright piano complete with soundboard and strings. Thomas recalls how he plucked those strings 'harp like fashion' until his fingers bled.

After some time he managed to get those old piano hammers to strike the strings in the ordinary way. He then attempted some form of tuning. Again he recalls "there was no theory about it; I only knew Do, Re, Me, Soh, etc. apart from this limited knowledge I had no other musical insight". He then began to teach himself tuning and simple playing technique. He knew nothing of 'equal temperament' and again he recalls "I tuned common Major chords as far as they would go for making a tune sound well in one key only. Later I needed to play in other keys, and met with difficulties. Amongst other

Westleigh Lane, Leigh, early 1900s. (Photo Wigan Record Office)

experiments, I tuned C to E a perfect Major third, the E and G sharp also perfect, and G sharp to the C above, perfect. The two Cs were then found to be amazingly out of tune with each other. I realised that three Major thirds must reach an octave, and the only way was to widen each interval equally until they did".

By this slow method Thomas had solved in a practical manner, the equal temperament problem before ever having heard of it. He also said: "My failure as a lad to obtain tone from a tight wire was in no way a set back — difficulties are made to be overcome, they are part of life's game".

It was to be some twenty-five years before he was to carry out further experiments of this nature, which were to lead to his specialization of string tone from wooden organ pipes.

Whilst working at Eatock Pits, Thomas found that he was out of work on a number of occasions during the strikes and disputes in the coal trade. In 1889 he was again out of work, the Eatock Pit closed and men did either casual work or wandered about the streets.

During the following year (1890), the Leigh Conservative Working Men's Reading Room, Leigh Free Library, The Co-operative Society and Leigh Literary Society gave books to a small library at a house in Kirkhall Lane, Leigh. These rooms were for the use of the strikers and the unemployed. The bulk of this library belonged to Mr. George Shaw, a local brewer who lived

Joseph Pendlebury, coachman, Westleigh Hall — brother of Thomas Pendlebury.

17

at Pennington Hall, Leigh. Amongst the books were many musical scores and books on Woodturning & Furniture Making for Amateurs, Violin & Clarinet Making, Gardening for Amateurs etc. They were the equivalent of our current D.I.Y. Magazines. No doubt Thomas read some of these publications as it was during a visit to this reading room that he came across a book entitled 'How To Build An Organ'. It was a book written for beginners and beautifully illustrated. Thomas, out of work, had time on his hands; he now began attempting to make wooden organ pipes. His workshop was a barn at his father's smallholding in Westleigh.

Along with his family, Thomas attended St. Paul's Church, Westleigh, here in 1892 he married a local girl Mary Hannah Twiss of Pennington. The marriage certificate states as follows:

St. Pauls Church	Westleigh: in the County of Lancaster: 1892				
Name	Age Status	Occupation	Date	Fathers Name & Occupation	
Thomas Pendlebury	25 Bachelor	Miner	Aug. 18	Robert Pendlebury (Farmer)	
Mary Hannah Twiss	20 Spinster	---	Aug. 18	David Twiss (Deceased) Tailor	

Mr. & Mrs. Thomas Pendlebury now took up residence at 152 Westleigh Lane; a property rented from Mr. Francis Hewart, shopkeeper, at a rent of 12s-4d per week (Rate Book 1893). Thomas must have again found work in the mines as the Marriage Certificate indicates. However in 1895 we see advertisements in which Thomas Pendlebury offers his services for tuning and renovating harmoniums and pianos. They now had a son James (later to follow his father as an organbuilder). The family of Thomas & Mary Hannah Pendlebury consisted of two sons and three daughters:

Thomas — Entered the organbuilding business for a time; later he left to pursue other interests. He was fluent in speaking 'Esperanto'. Later he became a draughtsman for British Aerospace.

Nellie — Entered the nursing profession. She also possessed a beautiful singing voice.

Constance — In later life became a landscape artist. She specialised in scenes of the Lake District and lived near Copper Mines Youth Hostel, Coniston. Her pictures were exhibited at the London Academy and in the Louvre, Paris. In the Catholic Church, Grasmere, Cumbria, the painted design on the sounding board over the Altar is her work.

Edith — Became a nurse. After her marriage she played the violin with an orchestra in Blackpool.

Thomas Pendlebury was now progressing into making organ pipes and also pieces of organ mechanisms; these examples of his work he took to organbuilders in the north of England, hoping for employment. In each instance he was rejected. Not having served an apprenticeship he was deemed unemployable. However, within a few years Thomas Pendlebury himself was employing organbuilders who were Union men, Pendlebury was to remark some years later: "It's only the boss who doesn't need an apprenticeship".

CHAPTER 3

Thomas
Pendlebury
1867–1933

THOMAS Pendlebury's first pipe organ was built in his cottage at 152 Westleigh Lane. All trace of this instrument has been lost. He then moved his workshop into the barn of his father's smallholding in Westleigh; shortly afterwards an opportunity arose in 1899 when the Trustees of Brunswick Methodist Chapel, Hindley Green, invited him to build an organ at a cost of £140. He had been tuning and maintaining their reed organ – harmonium – for some years. This was Thomas' first attempt to build for a place of worship. He had a little knowledge of carpentry and joinery and at one stage in its construction he admitted that he had a problem with the 'winding', stating: "I pondered over the problem for some hours, finally deciding to sleep on it. Later, I suppose I must have been semi-concious, I don't know, but I saw the problem ever so clearly. I didn't wait for daylight to break but went off to the barn, lit the paraffin lamps and completed the work".

The instrument he produced for Brunswick Chapel was a small but versatile organ consisting of one manual or keyboard, with eleven drawstops; six of which are half-stops down to Tenor C. (i.e. three-quarters of the keyboard). The remaining bass octave is taken care of by the Principal. Bourdon and Open Diapason stops are of full compass. Two stops, Dulciana and Voix Celeste, are enclosed in a small Swell Box which provides this instrument with a limited amount of expression. The pedalboard (a keyboard played by the organist's feet) was of a parallel and concave design, a style used by the German organbuilder Edmund Schulze; whose work was to have a great influence upon Pendlebury in later years.

Pendlebury's instrument was quite advanced for its date. He had built it upon a movable platform in order that it could be placed in any desired position. Tonally it produced a sound which was lively, bright and colourful, and whilst not attaining the quality of his later work, every stop is of musical interest. The casework too, is of good design for what is really a chamber organ; the pipework is not allowed to project beyond the tops of the side towers. Those pipes which make up the 'flat' (a set of pipes connecting one tower to another) are also trimmed to the curvature of the top rail, this rail is finished with a mould cut in the form of dentils. There is an attempt, albeit of rather heavy proportions, to provide pierced 'pipe shades' (mouldings following the tops of the pipes) in the side cases formed by the pedal pipes. The stop jambs whilst set well back are fixed at a convenient angle.

Many established organbuilders at this period were still producing instruments with straight stop jambs. All the casework cornices are finished with a moulding and the panel framework is bridle-jointed (a half mortice and tenon joint). The overall design has a sense of correctness and balance.

In 1979 Brunswick Chapel, Hindley Green, near Westleigh, was rebuilt. This delightful instrument was sold to St. Margaret's Catholic Chapel, Lytham Road, Blackpool, where the clergy are still very proud to be its custodians.

The earliest records kept by Thomas Pendlebury begin in 1897 with an entry for the Primitive Methodist Chapel, Daisy Hill, Westhoughton:

> To tuning American Organ 8s 0d.

1898. Brunswick Methodist Chapel, Hindley Green:

> To tuning pipe organ 12s 0d.

Specification for Brunswick Chapel, Hindley Green, Lancashire (1899), now in St. Margaret's Catholic Church, Blackpool:

Manual (Keyboard) CC-G. Pedals CCC-F

Left hand stopjamb.	Right Hand stopjamb
Open Diapason 8'	Rhor Flute 8' Tenor.C.
Stopped Diapason 8' Tenor.B.	Dulciana 8' Tenor.C. enclosed
Principal 4'	Voix Celeste 8' Tenor.C. enclosed
Super Octave Bass	Saube Flute 8' Tenor.C.
Super Octave Treble	Lieblich Bourdon 16' Pedal Organ &
Tremulant	Tenor.B. rank of stopped Diapason

Thomas Pendlebury's first organ and console (inset), built in 1899 for Brunswick Chapel, Hindley Green. Now in St. Margaret's Catholic Church, Blackpool.

The wooden pipes were hand made by Thomas Pendlebury who later specialised in this kind of pipework.

Another order was received early in 1900 to provide an organ for the Baptist Church, Church Street, Leigh. This was Thomas Pendlebury's first with some fifteen stops. A report of the Opening of the New Organ is recorded in the *Leigh Journal*, Friday 16th March 1900:

> "Leigh Baptist Church was crowded to capacity on Tuesday 13th March. The organ created by Mr. T. Pendlebury of 152 Westleigh Lane caused great interest. The recital was given by Mr. J. Charlton, M.A. Organist of Leigh Parish Church. The Committee who have had the matter in hand had the satisfaction of paying over the price of the instrument £220 the same evening. At the commencement of the recital, the Revd. R.D. Derby; Pastor of the Church; pointed out that Mr. Pendlebury is a native of Leigh, and entirely self taught, some seven or eight years ago he worked as a collier. Seven trades were supposed to be represented in organbuilding; but Mr. Pendlebury, with wonderful ingenuity had compressed them all and surmounted all difficulties. When a youth Mr. Pendlebury had studied and practised the construction of pianos, he also had leanings towards acoustics and harmony. Every part of the organ had been made by the builder, with the exception of some spotted metal pipes (metal organ pipes containing a high percentage of pure tin) and the ivory keys. The instrument had been partly built in his small workshop and other parts in his cottage".

The musical fare was comprised of transcriptions of popular items for the main section of the recital, nevertheless they brought some sort of musical appreciation to a public starved of such opportunities. The programme given at Leigh Baptist Church in 1900 followed these trends and it is interesting to compare the changes in musical tastes since the early part of this century:

> Programme given by Mr. J. Charlton, M.A. Organist of Leigh Parish Church:

Andante in G	Batioc
How Beautiful Are the Feet	G.F. Handel
Andante	Inglia Bervon
Triumphal March	M. Costa
Fugue in C Major	F. Mendelssohn
"Bells" Fuga in C Major	Bexfield
The Heavens are Telling (Creation)	J. Haydn
Hallelujah Chorus	G.F. Handel

> Solos by Miss Lizzie Rathbone of Leigh and Mr. J. Rowntree of Hindsford.

The Better Land
I Know That My Redeemer Liveth   G.F. Handel
Abide With Me   Liddel
The People That Walked In Darkness   G.F. Handel
Thou Art Passing Hence   Sullivan

Mr. Charlton responded with an encore 'Lift Up Your Heads' (Messiah) and the proceedings ended with the hymn 'Glory To Thee My God This Night'.

Thomas was now searching for premises away from his 'barn' workshop; and acquired two adjacent terraced houses Nos. 143 & 145 Glebe Street, Leigh. These he rented from Mr. Cowburn, a noted local building contractor who had carried out the brickwork for the fine building which is Leigh Town Hall; also the Alder Spinning Mill and several other notable buildings in the area.

Mr. & Mrs. T. Pendlebury now resided in one of these rented properties, the other which was without floors, was used as a workshop (Building Regulations and the Noise Abatement Act had not the complications we experience today). Thomas Pendlebury built a chamber organ for Mr. Cowburn and installed this in his house "The Grange" in Pennington, Leigh. Later this instrument was sold to an Italian; some years ago when Thomas' grandson, Stanley, was on holiday in Bolognia, it was found still giving regular service.

Numbers 143-145 Glebe Street, Leigh. Thomas Pendlebury's residence and workshop 1900-1908.

Mr. J. Cowburn seated at the Pendlebury organ in his music room, 'The Grange', Leigh (circa 1903). (Photo. Wigan Record Office)

Between 1900-1903 Thomas Pendlebury worked from his terraced houses in Glebe Street, Leigh. From here he built organs for:

1902 The Methodist Church, Westfield Street, St. Helens, Lancashire.

1903 The Baptist Church, Atherton, Nr. Manchester.

1904 Emanuel Methodist Chapel, Glazebury, Nr. Warrington.

1905 The Methodist Chapel, Bridge Street, Golborne, Nr. Wigan.

1906 St. Peter's Church, Hindley, Lancashire: Restoration of the famous Schulze organ.

1908 The Methodist Chapel, Daisy Hill, Westhoughton, Bolton.

From the Glebe Street workshop, Pendlebury, in later years, was to make an impact upon the Musical Press and the Organ World; and also in several other fields. For some years he had been influenced by the style of the great European organbuilder Edmund Schulze of Paulinzella, Erfurt, Germany. A fine example of this artist's work was placed in St. Peter's Church, Hindley in 1873. Hindley was only some two miles from Pendlebury's birthplace, there is strong evidence that he became acquainted with this instrument in his youth, for he became inspired by the Schulze tonal character, particularly the wooden pipes producing a strong string tone effect. A style he now adopted throughout his life.

The *Leigh Chronicle*, August 7th, 1903, stated:

ORGANBUILDER'S INVENTION

Mr. Thomas Pendlebury 143-145 Glebe Street, Leigh, Lancashire, the collier organbuilder, whose latest success is an improvement for the admission of wind into organ pipes. The invention recently patented "provides for a more satisfactory arrangement of membranes and tubes than hitherto provided for the admission of wind to organ pipes". Different methods are in use, but through various causes these arrangements are unsatisfactory. The Patentee claims this new method to be superior to any other device. It acts automatically and there is no possibility of it being affected by atmospheric change in the divisions of the windchest, or by falling dust. Mr. Pendlebury has been using this device for the last six years and he is fitting the new organ for the Atherton Baptist Church with this arrangement.

There is an interesting account relating to the early history of the Baptist Church in Atherton, the *Leigh Chronicle* May 16th, 1902:

"This building was proposed some ten years ago, but was shelved until half the cost had been raised, when it was opened free of debt. The edifice occupies a commanding position at the corner of Dan Lane, Atherton. It is designed to a cruciform plan of nave, transept, chancel, organ-chamber and vestries; with a western gallery arranged over the vestibule. The external walls are of Yorkshire par-points and red sandstone dressings. The roof is a collar-beam supported by Pitch Pine ornamental trusses designed on the hammer-beam principle.

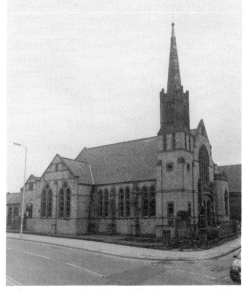

The internal woodwork is of Pitch Pine with the screens of English Oak. The architect was Mr. John B. Thornley of Darwen, Wigan & Blackpool; the builders Messrs. R. Rathbone & Sons of Atherton. The cost of the church was some £6,000.

The laying of the foundation stone began with a short service in the 'Elizabeth Burrows' Memorial School. The Burrows family have long associations with the Baptist Movement and are colliery owners in the township of Atherton. Mr. Moses Morris laid the foundation stone, remarking that "he re-

Atherton Baptist Church built 1902. Building replaced by modern church 1986-7. (Photo. Wigan Record Office)

Atherton Baptist Church interior and keyboards. (Photo. Wigan Record Office)

membered some seventy-years ago in 1832 the laying of the foundation stone for the 'old chapel'. He had never in all those years left the Baptist Chapel, except on one occasion when the Queen was crowned in 1837. He had done this because there were no 'buns' to eat at the celebrations.

Those who attended the Church Schools got a 'bun'. So many turned up that they had to cut the 'buns' into halves. I almost didn't get one, because someone said that a Baptist had no allegiance to the Queen".

The church was finally opened by Dr. Clifford of London; Mr. Miles Burrows placed the order for the new organ with Thomas Pendlebury, then a young and comparatively unknown organbuilder; having been established only a few years in the craft. He further demonstrated his confidence by giving the organbuilder an entirely free hand in the design and specification. Primarily designed for the support of hearty congregational singing, the accompaniment of numerous oratorios and some recital use; the instrument was not as complete as the builder would have wished. This was due to successive reductions in the amount of space available, and Thomas Pendlebury would never 'crowd' an organ. His soundboards were always of generous area, and every pipe had enough room to speak. Finance was no obstacle when this instrument was built, every metal pipe, including the two speaking fronts was of spotted metal (a mixture of lead and a high percentage of tin, giving a mottled pattern on the surface of the metal). The instrument occupied a chamber on the north side of the chancel, the pipe facades facing south and west. Apart from regular tuning and a small amount of maintenance this instrument gave trouble free service for forty-six years when it was re-built by Thomas' son.

This was Thomas' largest instrument to date, and he was justly proud of his success. He had attained a high standard of craftsmanship, he was a perfectionist, and demanded the same from others. During the installation of this instrument an employee slightly damaged one of the 'spotted metal' front pipes whilst carrying it into the building. He was sacked on the spot.

'Grand Opening Recital' on October 18th, 1903, was given by Mr. R.J. Forbes F.R.C.O., A.R.C.M. of Manchester. The Leigh Chronicle covered the event reporting that 'there was a capacity audience. Much had been heard about the superior quality of the instrument, and interest was also shown in the local builder Thomas Pendlebury.'

Some of the highlights from the programme were:

'Overture' from Tannhauser	Wagner
Cuckoo & Nightingale	G.F. Handel

Song "The Abiding City"	St. Quentin	
At Evening	Dudley Buck	
Grand Prelude & Fuge in A minor	J.S. Bach	
Grand Chorale in D (Style of Handel)	Guilmant	

Also included in the programme were vocal items by Madam Lizzie Rathbone, who was at her best on this occasion, finishing with an encore 'The Lost Chord'.

Pendlebury's instrument had a number of prominent features one of which was the 'Violin' stop; a specialization in which he was to become renowned, the tone of this stop closely followed the style of Edmund Schulze. The instrument was also unique in the number of pipes made entirely of wood, a speciality of the builder, the 'flute' toned pipes were also of a peculiar beauty. The design of the pedalboard (played by the organist's feet) was the builder's own idea. Pendlebury claimed that the feet of the organist did not make a true arc as they traversed the pedals, their movement was more eliptical with the middle five or six notes almost flat, this he claimed was a natural movement. The builder's 'patent' pneumatic system was also used in this instrument, an invention in 1903. The total number of pipes in the organ was 1,576.

Pendlebury's Letters Patent for the action which he invented and which he used on the above instrument were applied for on March 27th, 1903; and the Patent No. 7102 was granted on May 14th, 1903:

Atherton Baptist Church
Great Organ

Double Violin Diapason,	16 ft.	Wood and spotted metal
Open Diapson	8 ft.	Wood and spotted metal
Rohr Flute,	8 ft.	Wood Oak from tenor C up
Echo Horn (flue)	8 ft.	Spotted metal planed
Geigen Principal,	4 ft.	Wood and spotted metal
Twelfth,	$2^2/3$ ft.	Spotted metal
Fifteenth,	2 ft.	Spotted metal
Harmonic Trumpet,	8 ft.	Spotted metal
Swell to Great Coupler.		

Swell Organ

Violin,	8 ft.	Wood throughout
Violin Celeste,	8 ft.	Wood throughout
Gedacht,	8 ft.	Wood throughout
Corno Dolce,	8 ft.	Wood throughout

Salicional,	8 ft.	Wood string bass and metal above Middle C
Octave Violin,	4 ft.	Wood, top octave metal.
Fifteenth,	2 ft.	Spotted metal
Contra Fagotto,	16 ft.	Spotted metal
Cornopean	8 ft.	Spotted metal
Swell Octave Coupler.		Tremulant

Choir Organ

Open Diapason,	8 ft.	Spotted metal. (Unenclosed)
Clarabel Flute,	8 ft.	Wood (unenclosed)
Wald Flute,	4 ft.	Wood (unenclosed)
Harmonic Piccolo	2 ft.	Spotted metal (unenclosed)
Vox Angelica,	8 ft.	Spotted metal (enclosed)
Voix Celeste,	8 ft.	Spotted metal (enclosed)
Clarionet,	8 ft.	Spotted metal (enclosed)
Vox Humana,	8 ft.	Spotted metal (enclosed)
Tremulant		
Swell to Choir Coupler.		

Pedal Organ. All Wood

Open Diapason,	16 ft.	42 pipes
Violone,	16 ft.	42 pipes
Bourdon,	16 ft.	42 pipes
Pedal Octave Coupler.		
Swell to Pedal		
Great to Pedal		
Choir to Pedal.		

One of the last instruments to be built in the Glebe Street houses, was a small two manual instrument for the Methodist Chapel, Daisy Hill, Westhoughton, Bolton.

Thomas now received what transpired to be his most important commission, when in 1907 the authorities of St. Peter's Church, Hindley, Lancashire, requested him to restore the famous instrument, built in 1873 by Herr Edmund Schulze of Paulinzella, Erfurt, Germany. In business for only a few years, this was the opportunity that could either make or break Thomas Pendlebury. It was a challenge which he readily accepted. Thomas was very proud of his association with this instrument, and based his own tonal designs in the style of this European Artist.

Thomas Pendlebury carried out a thorough restoration at St. Peter's Hindley; replacing the old mechanical action with his own design of pneumatics on a low wind pressure. He retained all the original pipework, but carried out some re-voicing where necessary, thus retaining in essence the Schulze character. Pendlebury's pneumatic action gave reliable service for a further sixty-years. But in 1907, the award of this commission to an almost unknown organbuilder, created a storm of protest with many letters to the press and musical journals:

St. Peter's Church, Hindley, Lancashire

Sir,
The world of the organist is shocked by the events at Hindley, Lancashire. That a local man should be entrusted with this priceless instrument is nothing short of a public scandal. We the undersigned have written to the incumbent but without success meeting our cause. Like minded friends may feel obliged to do the same.

Signed Gore-Ousely
Dr. A.L Peace
Sir Walter Parrat.

This criticism centred around Pendlebury's modifications to this famous instrument. The arguments for and against these alterations continued for some years. The Revd. Noel Bonavia-Hunt, a prolific writer on the subject of organ construction and history; makes reference to the latter in his book 'The Modern British Organ'. He relates to a meeting with Thomas Pendlebury and quotes the builder admitting to making these modifications. The architect George Ashdown-Audsley, a native of Elgin, Scotland, published some thirty articles on organ design before emigrating to the U.S.A. in 1892. A man of scholarship, he wrote books on Oriental Art, Tastes & Fashions, Christian Symbolism and Painting & Architecture. His monumental work 'The Art of Organbuilding' was published in 1905, here Audsley outlines some progressive ideas, some of which were accepted by organbuilders. His criticism of Pendlebury's pneumatic invention was given in a professional manner, without malice or reference to Pendlebury's early beginnings. Other critics, however, never allowed him to forget his humble beginnings working in the mines. Bonavia-Hunt too, later gave Pendlebury high praise for his craftsmanship and compared him in some respects to the artist Edmund Schulze. There is also a record of Thomas Pendlebury supplying wood string pipes for an organ designed by the Revd. Noel Bonavia-Hunt. In later years those who had been his critics, began to take a different view. The professional musicians after giving recitals on instruments built by Pendlebury, held him in high esteem.

Thomas Pendlebury invited all his critics to the opening recital at St. Peter's Church, Hindley. Some did attend, several made return visits, gave him letters of recommendation and cultivated a friendship with the organbuilder. It was due to their influence that a number of important instruments contain pipes voiced by Thomas Pendlebury. One such instrument is the large concert organ in Radio City U.S.A.

(Note in archive of Wigan Record Office dated 1975):

'Yes sir'. The pipes are here and the plate of Thomas Pendlebury is inside the organ with them — very fine they sound and how well they keep in tune.

Signed Dr. Hartley-Boyd, Concert Director. (Radio City)

After the death of the renowned European organbuilder Edmund Schulze, a school of organbuilding was founded in England based upon the Schulze style. Thomas Pendlebury was included within its circle.

Now with increasing commissions Pendlebury required larger premises. But for the moment we must return to his birthplace in Westleigh, where two brothers William and James Hayes started work in Westleigh Mill (circa 1820). In 1836 they separated, William became one of the founders of the Cotton Doubling firm of Isherwood & Hayes. James moved from Westleigh Mill to Barlow's factory and there was joined by another brother John. Robert Thorp their brother-in-law now joined Isherwood & Hayes and from 1846 the firm was Thorp & Hayes. They employed some 110 people, the steam engine ran a twelve-hour day and the mill worked a sixty-nine hour week. The prosperity of the firm dates from the American Civil War 1861-65 which caused famine in Lancashire, due to a shortage of cotton. The Hayes family introduced new machinery and were pioneers in spinning Egyptian Cotton. They built homes for their employees and a Mission School to educate the workers' children, these buildings comprised Bedford Square, Leigh. The larger houses on Chapel Street, Leigh, were for their managers.

Some years later Thomas Pendlebury acquired the Mission School which was disused. This two storey building was ideal for his purposes with a gallery and large entrance door. Access to the upper floor was by an external staircase. There was also a small yard for storage. On the gable is a motif, a stone lion holding a sun in its paw, the border is inscribed EST SOLIS TESTIS (It is a witness of the sun). This building is still standing and one trusts it will be preserved.

The Edmund Schulze organ, built in 1873 and installed in St. Peter's Church, Hindley, near Wigan, Lancashire. After being in use for 33 years it was thoroughly overhauled, the voicing restored, and the old tracker action replaced by Tubular Pneumatic Action by Thomas Pendlebury, of Leigh, Lancashire.

A notice of the new premises appears in *Musical Opinion* 1908:

> Owing to a rapidly increasing business Mr. Thomas Pendlebury, Organbuilder of Leigh has removed to larger and more convenient premises in Bedford Square, Chapel Street, Leigh. The building which is a lofty one, heated by steam from the adjoining mills and has hitherto been known as Bedford Church Gymnasium.

Thomas Pendlebury now moved his residence to 182 Chapel Street, Leigh only a short distance from his newly acquired premises in Bedford Square. This dwelling had been one of the larger houses originally built as a manager's residence by Messrs. J. & J. Hayes Ltd.

He was now firmly committed to the tonal style of Schulze, in almost every instrument he built stops voiced with a strong string toned quality were introduced. He also began to expand upon the early experiments of his youth when he toyed with the strings of an old piano. Thomas recalls in later years: "In these experiments I stretched No. 25 gauge piano wire across a heavy circular saw bench, as being the most handy means of getting extra long strings in tension. The ends were secured to the lower framework, and the mechanical adjustment for raising the saw-bench table used to give whatever

J & J Hayes Mission School for their employees' children. Later the Old Gymnasium. Thomas Pendlebury's organ-building workshop in 1909. (Building still extant).

Interior of Thomas Pendlebury's workshop, Bedford Square, Leigh. The instrument under construction is for King Street Wesleyan Church, Leigh. (1909). (Photo Wigan Record Office)

tension I required. The strings were from 8-10 feet long. A triangular engineering file with the top edge ground smooth, this I placed under the strings near each end keeping them clear of the table. Without a soundboard the strings were almost toneless, but would vibrate for quite a long time when struck. To prevent any vibrations from the saw-bench tables, I placed bellows weights on them. A large thin soundboard was then made and placed under the strings, and a wooden bridge in contact with the strings replaced the engineering files. Now, when the strings were plucked, they gave the most wonderful string tone I had ever heard; one never tired of listening to just one note – the bass strings of a grand piano would not compare with it for beauty. This to me was 'Nature's Harmonious Chord'. It demonstrated the beauty of string tone, rich in pure multiple upper-partials and not 'damped' by the upper covering found on a piano.

I had learned an invaluable lesson. From uncovered string, the upper-partials were heard more clearly and pure than from a tone produced by other means. The ear did not ask that the 7th, 9th, 11th and 13th partials be eliminated or rendered softer. Many theorists, presuming to know better than NATURE think these partials should be eliminated. In nature's complete common chord, 'The Harmonious Senses' there is no roughness in any of the intervals. They are aliquot, there is no discordance between the parts. To play these notes on a tempered scale leads one away from the truth. Only as I heard them in my experiment, free and uncovered did I come to know them and they become part of oneself".

These notes of Thomas Pendlebury provide an insight of how he obtained his musical knowledge, his struggle to absorb information. He had no teacher; he relied upon his experiments and his skill as an innovator.

In the 'new' premises at Bedford Square, Leigh one of the first instruments to be built was a large three manual organ for the Wesleyan Church, King Street, Leigh. In 1909 this was a fine imposing building with a tall perpendicular spire. Internal arrangements for music consisted of a raised pulpit placed centrally and at a higher level the choir. To the rear was an arched organ chamber. A previous organ had stood there which was later sold to a Liverpool Church. On this gallery within the arch Pendlebury erected the new organ; the pipework was provided with a speaking 'gothic' frontal, the console was detached some distance from the pipes. And of course the action was his own 'patent' pneumatic action. The console (keydesk) was the first he provided with stopkeys (ivory tilting tablets engraved with the stop names, these moved vertically) rather than the traditional drawstops.

Thirty-seven of these stops were 'speakers' the remainder being couplers operating a movement to unite various sections of the instrument e.g. keyboard to keyboard or keyboard to pedals. Pendlebury also provided a generous supply of wooden pipework, and in an instrument of this quality his own speciality the 'violin' stop. All materials were of the best quality; timber absolutely 'free from knots and flaws' and windchests made of mahogany. Messrs. T. Vickerstaff & Co. Ltd. Timber Merchants & Saw Mill, Prescott Street, Leigh, supplied Pendlebury with selected hard and softwoods. Many of the wooden pipes were made of oak or mahogany these were varnished for protection. The moving parts to the windchests known as 'sliders' were 'black-leaded' for smooth and efficient action and the instrument contained 1,910 pipes. The Leigh Journal records some of the highlights of the 'opening' events – The instrument was dedicated and opened on Good Friday, April 6th, 1909, and a recital given by Dr. A.L. Peace, Esq. Mus.D., Oxon., F.R.C.O. City Organist of St. George's Hall, Liverpool. (Programme highlights):

Prelude & Fugue on the name B.A.C.H.	J.S. Bach
Sonata da Camera No. I. (D Major & minor)	A.L. Peace
Finale from the Organ Concerto in D	S.S. Wesley
Variations on an Old English Air	Sir Julius Benedict
Jubilee Overture	Weber
In the evening Dr. Peace accompanied a performance of 'Messiah' G.F. Handel.	

* * * *

The installation and opening of a new organ was an important event in any town or village in the earlier part of this century. Great interest was shown, not only by those for whom the instrument had been built; but full and detailed accounts were covered by the press whose imagination and enthusiasm was sometimes a little overdone. The flamboyant movements, rapid stop changes and pedalwork in many instances becoming more important than the music. Musical Journals gave accounts of the tonal quality and technical details of the instrument, and rival organbuilders took a keen interest in each others work.

This was an era without T.V., travelling orchestras, L.P. Recordings or cassettes. The only introduction to music for many were the popular songs of the time, for those fortunate enough to possess a gramophone with 78rpm records and a needle almost like a one-inch nail. In the cities too, the highlight of the week was the Saturday night organ recital at the Town Hall. They brought music to the people who would not have had the opportunity to enjoy it.

One can therefore imagine the excitement in Leigh when one of these showman performers, the well known concert organist David Clegg was invited to give a concert at the Wesleyan Church, King Street, Leigh. The *Leigh Chronicle*, September 1909 provides a detailed and colourful account of the proceedings:

"A large audience attended when the London recitalist David Clegg was invited to appear in Leigh. Mr. Clegg has now given over 3,000 recitals on instruments in all the principal cities of the British Isles, in Europe and also in America.

From the beginning he enraptured the crowd, and they listened spellbound during the performance that has probably never been excelled in the district.

On this occasion a splendid effect was conveyed by his interpretation of the London Queens Hall Carillon or (Celestial Bells). These were played from an adjoining room by Mr. Ronald Baker; the duet of organ and bells being very fine. Next was the 'Invocation to a Service at Lucerne Cathedral on a Festival Day' (Moritz). This work was in five parts (1) Celestial Chimes before Service; (2) Hourly Chimes; (3) Organ Voluntary; (4) Hymns with Voice effects; (5) Grand Fanfare of Trumpets. The bursts of melody mingled with the peal of bells, quite charmed the audience; the succession of beautiful sounds falling pleasantly upon the ear. Mr. Clegg then played the 'New Organ Symphony No. 6, this was executed with depth and brilliance

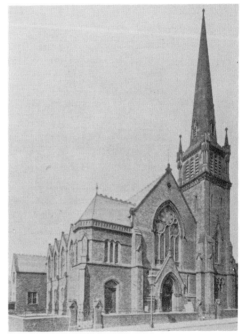

Leigh Wesleyan Chapel, King Street, Leigh. (Photo. Wigan Record Office)

38

The oak case, Gothic-style organ and surround installed at the Wesleyan Church, King Street, Leigh.

Three manual detached stopkey console built by Thomas Pendlebury for the Wesleyan Church, King Street, Leigh. (1909). (Photo. Wigan Record Office)

of style that excited the utmost imagination. But he rose to the greatest heights as a brilliant performer by his masterly rendering of Mendelssohn's "Finales" to the 3rd & 6th Sonatas. The manner in which he swept the keyboards in the Allegro movements, his wonderful pedal work; roused the audience to enthusiasm. The piano passages with their beautiful liquid music resembling the 'dance of the elves in the moonlight'; were linked sweetness drawn out. But when he arrived at the more majestic passages, in which the air "See The Conquering Hero Comes", Mr. Clegg played as one inspired; muscle and brain working together with the utmost harmony. Then he produced effects that would be incredible were they not plainly apparent to one's sense of hearing. It was organ playing in excelis.

There followed some improvisation on well known themes with the introduction of 'sweet chimes' as from a distant belfry. Then the strains of 'Jerusalem The Golden' with a reed effect sounding clear and pure, with a second effect as if a 'silver cornet' was playing the air with exquisite trills. Then came sounds as if the sweetest siffleur were whistling the melodic air along with nightingale and cuckoo effects, distant bells and the organ taking up the hymn tune "Pleasant Are Thy Courts Above". The sounds that we now heard were as if silver pebbles were dropping into a lake; more peals of bells, then from the organ the majestic chords of the harvest hymn 'We Plough The Fields and Scatter' followed by a roll of drums with the hymn tune in military band style fading away in the distance. The audience were enthralled and burst forth into a great cheer, which was again and again repeated.

David Clegg then played some modern transcriptions, a Bach Fugue and his own composition of Double Fugue in G Minor for Modern Organ on the Chorale "Leoni".

The finale to this event brought many of the audience to their feet as Mr. Clegg ended with his 'Storm in Switzerland'. – The opening music at first a peaceful setting indicating an open air concert held by Swiss peasants; the flutes and pipes giving way to the warbling of various bird songs. A dance takes place with drums and brass band, again the birds sing and the cuckoo joins in; then a low rumble. Flutes, pipes and birds continue, followed by more rumbles and effects of gusts of wind. A harsh reed note sounds, wind effects howl, followed by lighting and crashes of thunder increasing to violence, then dying away. The birds begin to sing again, the cuckoo calls and once more a fascinating sound of melody brought this work to a gentle close.

It was a wonderful feat of musical skill, and Mr. Clegg was given hearty applause, which he acknowleded by playing 'Home Sweet Home' with many variations. This recital was one of the greatest musical treats ever provided in Leigh. So many people had to be turned away at this first performance that Mr. Clegg was persuaded to repeat the recital the following evening, this he did to an overflowing audience."

From the press reports one could imagine that this was a much talked about event, and in some instances much enlarged upon. There was too, a great deal of 'artists licence' used in the programme; a style which won David Clegg large audiences. His programme in Leigh certainly made an impression, and many other organ recitals given on instruments built by Pendlebury were well attended; although they may have fallen short of the showmanship of David Clegg.

Shortly after these events Thomas Pendlebury received high praise from both recitalists Dr. A.L. Peace, City Organist, Liverpool and Mr. David Clegg, Concert Organist, London:

From the late David Clegg, Esq., Strand, London, W.C.
21 Buckingham Street, Strand, London, W.C.

Dear Mr. Pendlebury,

I intended sending you a line ever since my recital on your Leigh Wesleyan Organ, but being tossed about lately so much about the country and very busy upsets correspondence. I think your Leigh organ very praiseworthy. In some respects "unique". The organ is there in its solidity, dignified, yet on the top of it is the effect of a grand orchestra. I like particularly the wood gambas (violin and 'cello) effects. One might easily imagine it a real stringed orchestra instead of an organ. The wood-wind effects are also good. In fact, I compliment you sincerely in working out such a scheme, and I wish you continual success as you deserve.

Believe me, Yours very truly, David Clegg

Testimonial
From the late Dr. A.L. Peace, of St. George's Hall, Liverpool.

Dalmore, Blundellsands, Liverpool.
April 10th, 1909.

Dear Sir,

Will you allow me to express the great pleasure I have had in making the acquaintance of your workmanship in the excellent organ which I have just opened in the King Street Wesleyan Church, Leigh. Although I had previously heard good accounts of your work, I was hardly prepared for such a surprise—and I may add that I have rarely played upon an instrument that has afforded me so much real enjoyment. What struck me particularly was the beautiful quality and vitality you impart to the *basses* of your flue-stops—not in the case of one or two only, but to all of them—large or small.

I believe you are a follower in the school of Schulze. You certainly follow very closely on the heels of that famous builder. Your work has only to become known to extend your reputation far beyond the local surroundings of Leigh.

Yours faithfully,
A.J. Peace

David Clegg was Organist at Manchester University in the earlier years of this century. He also started a regular series of organ recitals at Salford Technical College (now Salford University).

The concert organ in the Winter Gardens, Blackpool was designed by David Clegg, it had many novel features; one such was a set of harmonium reeds fitted into resonators. Clegg commissioned various organbuilders to supply pipes, as he continually enlarged the instrument. His 'Celestial' organ was another curiosity, and was intended to reproduce the effects of ancient instruments as mentioned in the Psalms. Trumpets; Violas; Flutes; Reeds and Harp effects. To add to these Thomas Pendlebury supplied his special 'violin' pipes doubtless receiving this commission after the opening of the organ at King Street, Leigh.

David Clegg was considered a superb showman and a supremely gifted organist, a few critics remarked 'that after Clegg had opened an organ, it had to be repaired before it could be used again'. Nevertheless many people attending Clegg's recitals would remark on the various unusual effects that were heard from their new organ, and which had not been heard again. He did, however, take certain liberties in his programmes by placing the names of distinguished composers and performing music they had not written; and it must be admitted his concerts were designed to impress rather than to produce genuine organ music.

David Clegg enjoyed a tremendous reputation in his day at the Winter Gardens, Blackpool. During the season when the mill towns took their 'wakes week' holiday his audiences must have been extraordinarily large, and his showmanship and clever effects were impressive. These impressions would be carried back home; and when a new organ was to be opened, Clegg's name would immediately come to mind.

For fifteen years David Clegg gave endless pleasure to holidaymakers in the north of England. On his death this instrument was removed and later a more modern concert organ was installed.

From Dr. Alfred Hollins,
The world-famed (blind) Organist and Composer.

8 Grosvenor Street, Edinburgh.
12th May, 1911.

Dear Mr. Pendlebury,
I wish to tell you how much pleasure it gave me to make your acquaintance the other day, also to see your excellent organ at King Street Wesleyan Church, Leigh.

You are certainly a great artist in wood-pipe voicing; in fact, I have never heard finer wood stops than those in your organ at Leigh, especially the violin. The basses are wonderfully prompt and clear, and in a nonresonant building, this class of pedal tone makes florid passages come out much more distinctly. I found your action, too, very crisp and responsive.

With all good wishes for your continued success,
I am, Yours sincerely, Alfred Hollins, F.R.C.O.,
Organist, St. George's United Free Church, Edinburgh.

Mr. Frederick Boydell was appointed organist at the Wesleyan Church, Leigh. He held this post for many years, becoming somewhat of a local 'celebrity'. He ran a Music College & Artists Agency. Professor Boydell as he was known lived at the 'Hameland' 657 Leigh Road, Leigh; his home was named after a song he composed. The 'Hameland' is the last house on the left leaving Leigh on the Atherton-Leigh boundary. Madame Lizzey Rathbone who featured at many of the opening recitals of Pendlebury's organs, was Madame Lizzey Boydell.

Thomas Pendlebury's reputation as an organbuilder and also as a voicer was now established. He was supplying his string toned pipes to other builders in the trade, no doubt to some of those who in earlier days had turned him away. His style was now acclaimed in standard text books on organ construction and history. Those who had earlier condemned him now acknowledged him as a craftsman. In the *Musical Opinion* journal 1908-9, Thomas Pendlebury advertises his 'wood pipes of Diapason, String & Flute tone'. There must have been a demand for these wooden pipes, for in a later advertisement we see N.B. 'The special wood stops are not for sale separately as the supply is limited and all are required for the new organs continually in building'. – Bedford Square, Leigh, Lancashire.

It would seem that his competitors wished to obtain ranks of pipes voiced by Pendlebury; these for inclusion into their own schemes, and without giving any credit to their maker.

From the Rev. Noel A. Bonavia-Hunt, M.A.,
Author of "Studies in Organ Tone", etc.

21 Hillingdon Road, Uxbridge, Middlesex.
May 17th, 1913.

Dear Sir,
The pipes arrived yesterday, and I am greatly pleased with them. The tone is very fine and they match the metal pipes most successfully. I am very grateful to you for doing them.

Yours very truly,
Noel Bonavia-Hunt.

In "STUDIES IN ORGAN TONE" Mr. Hunt mentions "that remarkable tone production of Mr. Thomas Pendlebury's" which he calls his 'wooden violin'. In Mr. Hunt's opinion, "Mr. Pendlebury's creation is the nearest approach to real violin tone yet attained from any organ pipe, and in many respects it is one of the most noteworthy achievements of modern organ tone. The tone is broad and pungent, and yet retains the mellowness and refinement which is so essential to a succesful imitation of the violin. To appreciate its full beauty it must be heard as a solo stop in a swell box with a slow beating tremulant; but the effect in chords is extraordinarily rich and telling. The tone of the bass and tenor octaves is magnificent, while the treble octaves are equally effective. The stop is constructed in wood throughout, and is the first successful attempt at wooden viol tone above middle C."

In the same book, writing of Pendlebury's Wood Diapasons, Mr. Hunt says he "can unhesitatingly certify to the superb tonal effect of this artist's pipe-work, but it is very probable that the amount of patience and skill needed to reproduce Mr. Pendebury's tone may discourage any attempt at imitation on the part of the average student".

From R. Meyrick-Roberts, Esq.

Organist of St. Mary-le-Boltons, S.W. (Formerly of the American Church, Paris); and Organist and Choirmaster of the (St. Paul's) National Welsh Festivals.

48 Waldemar Mansions, Fulham, S.W.
August 22nd, 1909.

Dear Mr. Pendlebury,

I must write a few lines just to tell you how very thoroughly I enjoyed playing upon your fine organ at the King Street Wesleyan Chapel. I had already heard favourable accounts of the instrument, but an acquaint-ance with it not only confirm what I had heard, but gave me even more pleasure than I had anticipated.

The general effect of the organ I considered to be excellent in tone quality, power, and balance; the diapasons very fine and Schulze-like; but the string-toned wood-stops were a complete surprise to me, particularly in regard to the power and volume of tone you have obtained. They are the finest I have met with.

The mechanism and action appeared, after the trying test of a long recital, to be all that one could desire.—With congratulations,

Believe me, Yours sincerely,
R. Meyrick-Roberts.

From King Street Wesleyan Church, Leigh.

April 11th, 1910.
Mr. Pendlebury,

Dear Sir,

On behalf of the Trustees of the King Street Wesleyan Church, Leigh, we desire to convey to you their very sincere thanks and appreciation

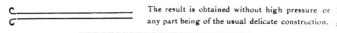
Musical Opinion 1909

of the manner in which you have carried out the designing and erection of the New Organ built by you for this church.

The voicing and tone of the instrument, together with the touch and promptitude of the tubular pneumatic action, are in every way most satisfactory; various competent organists who have had the pleasure of examining and trying the instrument are unanimous in their praise of these features. The bellows and blowing arrangements, too, are ample and efficient, the triple-action feeders being operated by an electric motor of special design and with auto-governor combined (by Messrs. W. Boydell & Sons, of Leigh), which during the past year have worked most economically without the slightest hitch whatever.

The Sub-Committee appointed by the Trustees for the purpose of carrying out the various matters are of the opinion that the workmanship and design are in every way worthy of their commendation, and desire to express the great pleasure the many interviews and consultations have given them, they having always found you most courteous, obliging, and ready to assist them in every possible way.

The instrument having been in use for a year and subjected to various severe tests, nothing whatever of any moment has needed your attention. The Trustees, therefore, in completing settlement, resolve to ask your acceptance of a small honorarium (20 guineas) in addition thereto, to mark their appreciation of your worthiness, and on their behalf,

We are, dear sir, Yours respectfully,

J.J. Smith, Minister.

John Calvert, Secretary.

A commission was now received to build an organ for the Wesleyan Chapel, Elliot Street, Tyldesley. This chapel had a spacious archway providing the builder with a wide layout. Pendlebury favoured large areas in which to erect his instruments. The Tyldesley instrument consisted of two manuals (keyboards) and pedals (played by the organist's feet) and twenty-nine drawstops, the case was made of selected Pitch Pine.

The *Leigh Chronicle*, 1909, covered the opening events which comprised two recitals: Wednesday September 1st given by Mr. Caradog Roberts, Mus.B., F.R.C.O., of Ross Ruabon; with vocal artists Miss Kathleen Smith, (Soprano) of Tyldesley and Mr. Arthur Webber (Bass) of Liverpool Cathedral; and on Sunday September 5th a recital was given by Dr. R.H. Mort Mus.B., F.R.C.O., Organist of Atherton Parish Church. It was reported that the recitals differed greatly in style. That given by Mr. Roberts was more of a concert with transcriptions and concluding with an organ arrangement of the Hallelujah Chorus (Handel). Whilst Dr. Mort's recital consisted of classical items. Again

Thomas Pendlebury was given high praise for his workmanship in a letter from Mr. Caradog Roberts:

From Mr. Caradog Roberts, Mus. Bac. Oxon, F.R.C.O., A.R.C.M., L.R.A.M.
Mount View, Rhos, near Ruabon, N. Wales.
September, 8th, 1909.
   I have great pleasure in stating that I consider the New Organ erected by Mr. Thomas Pendlebury at the Wesleyan Chapel, Tyldesley, to be an excellent specimen of organ-building in every respect. The tone is of a full and rich quality, while the pneumatic action is very prompt.
Yours faithfully,
Caradog Roberts, Mus. Bac. Oxon, F.R.C.O., A.R.C.M., L.R.A.M.

When the Wesleyan Chapel, Tyldesley closed this fine instrument was sold to the Catholic Church of St. Gregory The Great, Preston where it still gives regular service.

   In 1910 the internal arrangements for Astley Methodist Church, near Manchester were the results of an architectural 'blunder'; no provision had been made for the installation of a pipe organ. The Trustees invited Thomas

The pitch pine Renaissance-style case at the Wesleyan Church, Tyldesley. (Photo Wigan Record Office)

Pendlebury to build an organ for them. Pendlebury on visiting the church remarked: "I find that an organ built so that the tuner can get at everything is easier to maintain and cheaper to run. In some organs it costs £20 to get a 5s (25 new pence) worth of work". After this instrument was completed the authorities of Astley Methodist Church complimented the builder on overcoming a difficult situation by presenting him with £20 over and above the cost of the instrument.

In the same year another fine instrument left the workshop in Bedford Square, Leigh; this for St. John's Parish Church, Hindley Green, near Wigan. This organ of two manuals and pedal with twenty-one stops is fitted into an archway on the north side of the chancel. Here we have the first reference of Thomas Pendlebury working in collaboration with church architects. The oak frontal for this instrument was designed by Messrs. Austin & Paley of Lancaster (architects) and executed by Messrs. Hatch & Sons (Carvers) of Lancaster.

The materials for this instrument were of the very best selected pine and mahogany, the console handsomely finished in oak. The action was the builders 'patented' system. The instruments wind supply in 1910 was with the aid of an hydraulic engine; these engines were made by Messrs. W. Boydell & Sons, Engineers & Ironfounders, Brown Street, Leigh. The instrument is still in regular use, and was restored some years ago by Thomas' grandson, Stanley, who retained its character just as his grandfather had left it with its original pneumatic action, but replacing the hydraulic engine with an electrical fan blower.

Thomas Pendlebury was particularly fond of the Lake District. He must have received with delight the commission from the Trustees of Keswick Methodist Church, to build an organ for them in 1911. Pendlebury placed the casework and console which was detached, at the front behind the choir. The action he introduced was of course his 'patent' system. In this design he placed the drawstops directly above the Swell manual (upper keyboard); and when the author visited this instrument it was still giving trouble free service after some eighty years. The organ produces a solid vigorous sound with individual stops giving beautiful solo voices. Pendlebury up to this time still was not introducing 'Mixture' stops into his tonal schemes (a stop sounding other than its unison or one of its octaves). Indeed, in the full choruses of Pendlebury's instruments one does not really miss them; always claiming that as he had included enough harmonics (overtones) into his individual stops, 'mixtures' were unnecessary.

Due to his love of the Lake District, Thomas Pendlebury would personally travel to Keswick in order to tune this fine instrument. Thomas' car was a

The oak case, gothic-style organ installed at St. John The Evangalist's Church, Hindley Green, near Wigan. (Photo. Wigan Record Office)

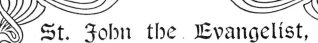

St. John the Evangelist,

HINDLEY GREEN.

Dedication of the - - # New Organ,

.... ON .....

WEDNESDAY, JAN. 26, 1910, at 7-30,

BY THE

LORD BISHOP OF LIVERPOOL.

ORGAN ⊕ RECITAL

after service by :: ::

E. C. Robinson, Esq., Mus. Bac., F.R.C.O.,

Organist of Wigan Parish Church.

A RECITAL will also be given on Sunday Afternoon, Jan. 30, at 3-0,

——— BY ——— -

MR. R. GREENOUGH, Organist of St. John's,

- - and on - -

Wednesday Evening, February 2, at 7-30,

there will be a

Recital by J. Martin, Esq., F.R.C.O.,

Organist of Wingates Parish Church.

**THE OFFERTORIES AT THE ABOVE RECITALS WILL BE
TO DEFRAY EXPENSES, AND TO PROVIDE
NEW SURPLICES FOR THE CHOIR.**

Rudd Bros., Printers, Hindley.

Programme frontispiece 1910.

Calthorpe; and he would frequently allow his sisters to accompany him to the Lake District when tuning.

Pendlebury's car was regularly serviced at Gerard's Garage, Mather Lane, Leigh. Thomas was very interested in mechanics and had modified the *Calthorpe*, particularly the braking system and gears. He was very critical of 'shoddy work' – there were to be no fingerprints or oil stains after a service even in the engine compartment.

An ex-native of Leigh Mrs. Lily Edwards, now living in Lancaster, was a neighbour of Thomas Pendlebury in Chapel Street. She was then Miss Lily Hull, her father was Joseph Hull, F.R.C.O., Organist of the Wesleyan Church, King Street, Leigh and a well known recitalist in the area. Joseph Hull also worked for Thomas Pendlebury for a time, assisting in the erection of organs together with officiating as a recitalist. Miss Lily Hull married a clergyman of the Methodist Church. After leaving Leigh she lived for some years in Jamaica and later in Paris. She remembers a trip with her mother to stay in the Lake District, when her father was working for Pendlebury, erecting the organ in Keswick Methodist Church in 1911 and states: "The journey was made by

Thomas Pendlebury driving his 'Calthorpe' motor car on a 'tuning' visit to Keswick in the Lake District. His son (James) is the passenger seated beside him. (Photo Wigan Record Office)

charabanc, a motor bus which had solid wheels and hard wooden seats. I and my mother made the journey as far as Grasmere, but the remainder of the trip had to be made by horse drawn conveyance". She recalls too, that Thomas Pendlebury's hobby was growing tea roses. "On Saturday evenings Mr. Pendlebury would call for a game of whist, and would bring a tea rose for my mother, which he would produce from under his bowler hat. He would then join some friends at an eating house in Leigh for steak and kidney puddings. He would talk very intensely about organbuilding, he had a blunt nature, which could turn to great kindness".

Between 1909-21 Pendlebury built fifteen instruments, from Keswick in the west to Richmond in Yorkshire. He had received fulsome praise from many leading musicians and had triumphed over their earlier criticisms.

But what sort of a man was Thomas Pendlebury? I expect all 'geniuses' are a little difficult to get along with. He was more of an artist than an accountant; making large profits was unimportant to him. His background created a manner of approach which to some people sounded rather direct. He once told some Chapel Trustees who asked him: "Mr. Pendlebury, what does our organ require?" He replied by suggesting that they provide some paraffin, and he would supply the match. When the Vicar of Leigh, a noted high churchman visited the Wesleyan Church, Leigh, to hear the organ built by Pendlebury, the vicar remarked that "he supposed any organ would sound

The console Keswick Wesleyan Church.

53

The beautiful gothic-style case at Keswick Wesleyan Church.

well in a market hall" infuriated the organbuilder. When some work was required to be carried out to the Leigh Parish organ, Pendlebury refused to consider him as a client.

Some of Pendlebury's employees remember that he could change from biting criticism with a threatening of the 'sack' for dropping an organ pipe – to almost excessive paternalism. He was very helpful to young people and would encourage their inspection of an organ.

A local man living near Bedford Square, Leigh, remembers how Thomas Pendlebury would invite the young lads who played around the area into his workshop to show them what was being built and how it worked. He would encourage them to ask questions and invite them again when the instrument was finished. His paternalism however, did not always extend to his family, and it was felt, at least by some of the locals in the Bedford Square area, that at times he was difficult and neglected his family, when living with a mistress from time to time.

Thomas Pendlebury was a perfectionist and demanded the same of others particularly from those in his employment. The transportation of an organ from workshop to church was planned meticulously by him. He is remembered as "being a little on edge at these occasions, as every move had to be made in an orderly and tidy manner. It was heaven help anyone who didn't toe the line". William Hesford, whose father was a Furniture Remover in Leigh, tells of the work they obtained moving organs for Pendlebury's: "All the vans and horses were brought to the workshop in Bedford Square, Leigh, on the previous evenings and loaded up. The following morning after feeding at first light, they would move off in convoy; some horses in pairs others in single shafts. On arrival at the church they would be lined up outside the Lytch Gate or West Door; again the orderly business of unloading with Thomas Pendlebury directing operations would be carefully carried out".

A similar scene must have presented itself outside St. Paul's Parish Church, Westleigh in 1914. A number of horse drawn vehicles, the animals' brasses gleaming would give this a sense of occasion. Thomas Pendlebury returning to the church he had once attended as a boy with his family, where he married; and where he would later be laid to rest. Here he came in 1914 to build what is in the author's opinion his finest work.

In this instrument for the first time Pendlebury introduces the 'Mixture' stop on the Swell keyboard (uppermost keyboard). Comparing this instrument with earlier and also later examples it outshone them all. It is positioned on the south side of the chancel in a casework of selected Pitch Pine.

Everything about this instrument is of the highest order, from mechanism to tonal quality. The pipework is laid out with ample speaking room, the wooden pipes are varnished for protection, and the windchests on which they stand are of best mahogany. The sliders (mechanical movements in the windchests) and also the 'blocks' forming the pipe mouths (apertures from which the wooden pipes speak) these are black-leaded. A practice Pendlebury carried out with thoroughness. The console is made of English Oak, with keys and stop heads of best ivory. The pneumatic-action between keys and windchests is Pendlebury's own 'patent' action; both this and the stop movements are as smooth and crisp as when new. The selected hardwoods used in the construction of this instrument and that of its wooden pipes, are Oak, Mahogany, Teak, Kauri and Maple. The metal pipes consist of 50% tin and lead. Included also is Pendlebury's special 'Violin' stop. The voicing of the pipework is superb. And the 'full swell' effect with its 'Mixture' and double reed Corno di Bassetto 16ft provides a glorious 'cathedral' roll effect in the full chorus. The instrument is tuned to Harmonic Pitch.C.522.

The dedication of this organ at St. Paul's, included two recitals, the first was given at the Dedication, when the Revd. J. Bamber M.A., Rector of Didsbury, took as his text 'Let Everything That Hath Breath, Praise The Lord'. received the instrument on behalf of the church. A recital was also given by Dr. R.H. Mort, Mus.D., F.R.C.O. Organist of Atherton Parish Church. A report appears in the *Leigh Journal & Times*, Friday November 13th, 1914:

> On the whole this recital was disappointing, the performer evidently labouring under the difficulty of insufficient acquaintance with the instrument in order to bring out to the best advantage the various tonal colours. That this was the case was obvious to all present by the long pauses made at many points, in order to effect the most ordinary stop changes. Moreover, the results of these pauses was to utterly destroy the musical sense and there was an entire lack of connected musical rhythm or artistic phrasing. The loss of which was not redeemed by the apparently interminable final chord. This latter did, however, give the audience an opportunity of admiring the magnificent tone of the full organ, in which the various families of Diapason, Reed, String and Flute tones are heard in perfect balance. A collection for the organ fund amounted to £9 and the event ended with the singing of the National Anthem.
>
> Recital by Dr. R.H. Mort D.Mus. F.R.C.O.
>
> | | |
> |---|---|
> | Chorale Song & Fugue | S.S. Wesley |
> | Harmonies due Soir | Karg-Elert |

Fantasia pour Orgue	Saint-Saens
Chasson de Nuit	E Elgar
Allegretto	Niels W Gade

There followed on November 27th a recital given by Mr. Joseph Hull, Organist & Choirmaster, Wesleyan Church, Leigh. The *Leigh Chronicle* gives an account of this event:

"As one of the most instructive and interesting recitals it has ever been our privilege to hear. St. Paul's was full to capacity, to hear a well chosen programme, listened to with rapt attention. On this occasion Mr. Hull not only maintained but improved the reputation he gained years ago, that of being an all round brilliant recitalist. One of the characteristics of his playing is his solidity and strict tempo when full organ is used. Another aspect of Mr. Hull's playing is that in brighter pieces when much rapid changes of stops are required, he invariably makes these without a pause in the rhythm. That is as it should be, for in our own opinion, to pause every few bars in order to change stops is intolerable. In the entire programme his choice and blending of tone was most creditable. The magnificence of the full organ was heard in Mendelsshon's Sonata No. 4. The builder's special wood string stop, the 'Violin', came out well in Schubert's Ava Maria; Guilmant's Prayer and Cradle Song and Mendelsshon's 'I Waited For The Lord' were performed with beautiful contrasted tone colours. Air and Variations (Haydn) and the tone picture 'At Evening' (Dudley-Buck) displayed the performer's powers of expression; his blending of Flute, Reed and String was beyond criticism. The concluding item was Finale Grande Chorus No. 198 (Lemmens). The first and last movements were a study in brilliant staccato and full organ, which were performed with clarity and firm technique."

At the close of the recital the organbuilder was heard to remark: "The organ had

Advert from Leigh Chronicle: Hesford transported many organs for Thomas Pendlebury by horse drawn conveyance (circa 1912). (Photo. Wigan Record Office)

Some of the men employed by William Hesford who transported Pendlebury organs by horse-drawn conveyance (circa 1912). (Photo Wigan Record Office)

been handled exactly as it was designed to be".

Thomas Pendlebury now brought out what he termed the '2 manual - three organ'. He describes this instrument in a booklet published in 1928: "It is the next best thing to the much desired three manual (keyboard) instrument where funds are low and room is limited. It also overcomes the shortage of soft accompaniment stops on the Great manual (lower keyboard) to go with the Swell (upper keyboard) solo stops. In the organ built by us practically every stop on the Swell is a solo stop of very definite character, and all tonal character is not confined to the everlasting Oboe stop. In fact there is so much diversity of tonal character in our Flute stops that in many cases we omit the Oboe in our tonal schemes.

In this model there was a mechanism to provide for quick changes of stops by a series of metal foot levers placed above the pedalboard. If stops on the Great Keyboard are in use and a tonal change was required to the Choir organ section on the same keyboard, the first lever takes 'off' the stops in use and puts into use a Flute and String also reducing the Pedal Organ to a quiet register. If a 'coupler' is in use, this is also taken 'off' without removing the

St. Paul's Parish Church, Westleigh and organ built by Thomas Pendlebury in 1914. (Photo. Wigan Record Office)

hands from the keyboards. One of these instruments was built for Blackrod Methodist Church, Lancashire, in 1921. When this church closed the instrument was installed in St. Benedict's Catholic Church, Hindley, Wigan.

The tonal schemes of Thomas Pendlebury were based on a few carefully chosen stops, from these he developed others providing his instruments with a plethora of tonal colours. He claimed too, that the tone produced by him from these few stops was totally different in both power and quality from those found in other instruments bearing the same designations. Thomas Pendlebury describes his creations thus:

Major Bass	A powerful stop of large scale (width & depth) and the chief foundation tone for the Pedal section of our organs. It has great dignity and depth of tone.
Open Diapason	This is the true Diapason, a full, rich, warm pervading tone. The bass end of the compass is made from wooden pipes, the remainder of metal.
Violone	This tone is brilliant and powerful. It has great distinctness in the Pedal section; useful in Fugal work and rapid pedal passages.
Giegen Diapason	This is our foundation tone for a large Swell organ. It is rich in the bass and brilliant when played in chords.
Violin	Called 'Cello' & Violin; a small scaled stop it adds brilliance to the Swell organ. It is the most notable of all my creations. When played an octave lower than its unison, as a solo, it is a real 'cello' in quality. It will also remain in tune in extreme temperatures.
Viol Celestes	These are two ranks of violins tuned as a Celeste, giving a most extraordinary effect of vibrating strings.
Rhor Flute.	This has a distinct character with its odd number of harmonic partials as clearly brought out as possible. It is louder and more refined than the metal stop of the same name. It forms a useful solo stop, the quality of tone is mid-way between an orchestral Clarinet and Flute. We used to make these stops of Oak but now prefer Mahogany.
Corno Dolce	The tone of this stop is a little brassy in the lower octaves and as the scale ascends changes to a smooth horn, then to a flutey quality in the treble. It is an imitation of an Orchestral Horn played softly. The beauty is in the changing tone colour in the scale.
Wald Flute	This is a variation of the Corno Dolce but is much brighter in character.

Echo Horn This is a special metal stop, but is worth a mention here. It is different from any other metal stop known to me. And again the beauty is in the change of tonal colour as the scale ascends from a rich soft warm Horn in the bass octave, to a full flutey tone at the top of the compass.

Our metal pipes we do not make ourselves. I always obtain either Spotted Metal of good substance or Hand Rolled Zinc. Plain metal is unsuitable for large pipes, as it is too soft to stand on its own weight for any length of time. Where funds are not sufficient to provide for the use of spotted metal, zinc is the next preferable metal. For other pipes such as Salicional, Aeoline, Viol di Gamba, Voix Celestes, Vox Angelica, Dulciana there is nothing better than 'spotted metal' (a mixture of lead with a very high percentage of pure tin. During the cooling process large irregular spots form on the face of the metal, forming a pleasing pattern and also providing a brighter tone than plain organ metal). This I use from the Tenor.C. pipe upwards in the scale.

The above shows Thomas Pendlebury's inner vision as he describes the tones he hears in colours and his sensitivity to the variation in aural sounds when he prefers Mahogany to English Oak for some of his flute stops.

And again Pendlebury remarks on some contemporary schemes of the period: "It isn't a change of strength or power that is required. It is a change of tonal colour".

Between 1910-1931 Pendlebury had built organs for:

1910 St. John's Parish Church, Hindley Green, Wigan.
1911 The Methodist Church, Keswick, Cumbria.
1912 The Methodist Church, Richmond, Yorkshire.
1914 St. Paul's Parish Church, Westleigh, Leigh, Lancashire.
1914 St. Anne's Parish Church, Warrington.
1914 The Methodist Church, Wigan Road, Leigh, Lancashire.
1917 Mount Zion Methodist Church, Pemberton, Wigan.
1919 The Methodist Church, Cook Street, Leigh, Lancashire.
1919 The Methodist Church, Kendal Street, Wigan. (Installation of the Samuel Renn Instrument from All Saints Church, Hindley).
1920 The Methodist Chapel, Coppull, Chorley.
1920 The Winter Gardens Palace, Blackpool. (Special wood violin stop added to David Clegg's concert organ).
1920 The Methodist Church, Ainsdale, Southport.
1920 (circa) Radio City, U.S.A. Concert Organ (Special wood strings Pendlebury's Violin stop).
1921 The Methodist Church, Bedford, Leigh, Lancashire.

1921   The Methodist Chapel, Blackrod, Rivington, Lancashire.
1923   The Methodist Church, Stockton Heath, Manchester.
1926   The Congregational Church, Market Street, Farnworth, Bolton.
1927   The Methodist Chapel, Starcliffe, Bolton.
1929   The Sacred Heart Catholic Church, Leigh, Lancashire.
1930   St. Joseph's Catholic Church, Leigh, Lancashire. (Rebuild).
1931   The Congregational Church, Market Place, Wigan. (Rebuild).

* * * *

The inventiveness of Thomas Pendlebury extended beyond his craft as an organbuilder. He designed and patented improved safety guards for wood-working machinery. In 1923 before the advent of the Ministry of Transport Driving Test, he had invented and patented a dual control system for the motor car, whereby a learner driver could be taken on the highway with an added degree of safety.

In 1928 Pendlebury provides some further opinions on tonal designs: "in voicing some of my pipes, I take for example what is the most reasonable and satisfying qualities of tone for the bass and treble to imitate – the work of the Creator – human voices. These are rich in upper partials in the treble. In fact to my sense of hearing – from FF in the bass to treble F, three octaves, every note seems to be of a slightly different tone colour, a gradual changing from richness to flutiness. I can think of no better way of classifying this, than to say it is Naturally Balanced."

"From my earliest recollections the study of tone colours has always been of fascinating interest, no matter whether they were the human voice, strings, reeds, flutes, drums, organ pipes or anything that was musical."

"When I first became acquainted with organ stops, for instance, the Open Diapason – its one peculiarity that distinguishes it from all other instruments, its beauty, was at once noticeable to me. Why do so many organists never use the Diapason on its own? Is it due to the fact that they have been acquainted with too many examples lacking brightness in the bass octave? Anyone with the slightest knowledge of 'voicing pipes' can produce a dull humming bass from flue pipes, but to obtain the various shades of string and reed tones in the bass requires an artist. Spend your money on the bass end of the organ, screaming whistles are cheap. It is at the expensive end of the keyboard, the bass, that I am ever striving to improve. In my early days I followed the example of others and included Sub-Octave Couplers in order to improve the lower end of the keyboard but I never heard a really good organist use them. Now I never include a Sub-Octave on the same manual (keyboard) it is not artistic. Have you heard the fifths and fourths produced by them? It offends the ear; study your harmony".

These are the thoughts and ideas of a man from a humble background, a man who had struggled to obtain knowledge, who had withstood the criticisms of his contempories and was finally held in esteem by those who had denigrated him.

During the closing years of his career he produced four further examples of his art. A large three manual instrument with a stop-key console for the Congregational Church, Market Street, Farnworth, Bolton. And a fine example for the Sacred Heart Catholic Church, Leigh. This building was opened with unofficial ceremony in 1929, it is a fine example in Red Brick and Darley Dale Stone dressings in the Early English Style. The new organ built by Thomas Pendlebury, the gift of an anonymous donor, is positioned in the western gallery. The pipe frontal and console is in English Oak. Examination of this instrument revealed that to the end of his career Pendlebury retained the highest standards of workmanship. The pipework is laid out with ample room for tuning and maintenance; the soundboards on which the pipes stand are of best Mahogany. The large bass 16 ft. pipes of the Pedal Organ were found to be absolutely free from knots and defects and are of selected Douglas Fir. The tonal quality of the stops is as described by Thomas Pendlebury and ideally fit the building. The instrument was originally blown by an hydraulic engine manufactured by Messrs. T. Boydell, Engineers & Ironfounders, Brown Street, Leigh. Some years ago an electrical fan blower superseded this mechanism. The hydraulic engine was left intact. It still remains in its original position, complete with leather cogged drive belt, and is a fine example of a bygone age of local engineering.

The following year 1930, Pendlebury was invited to rebuild the organ in St. Joseph's Catholic Church, Leigh. This instrument had stood in Bromsgrove Parish Church until 1858 and contains some historical pipework by Elliott; who was, for a time, in partnership with the great English organbuilder William Hill. Messrs. John Nicholson of Worcester later rebuilt the instrument and installed it in St. Joseph's. The installation was celebrated on November 13th, 1858 with the newly formed brass band, vocal selections by Miss Honiker of Manchester who also accompanied on the German Flautina, there were also hand-bell ringers and glee singers.

In 1930 Pendlebury considerably rebuilt this instrument adding a third manual (Choir Organ) together with modifications to the specification and action.

Thomas Pendlebury's 3 manual detached console in St. Joseph's Catholic Church, Leigh. (1930).

Thomas Pendlebury's 'swan song' was the restoration of the instrument in Hope Congregational Church, Market Place, Wigan. His son James now took a larger share of the workload. Thomas' health had begun to fail. In 1931 he entered hospital for what was really a minor operation; but during his stay in hospital his strong personality and forthright character pulled him through. In his determination to recover, he had 'sacked' the doctors telling them: "any mistakes he had made during his life he had to live with. The mistakes they made were buried in the churchyards". Sometime later his health again deteriorated and he became a sad, sick man confined to an invalid chair but never lost his great enthusiasm to talk about his art to anyone ready to listen.

In the latter part of the nineteenth century a school of organbuilding was formed based upon the style of the great European artist Edmund Schulze of Paulinzella, Erfurt, Germany. This school included James Jepson Binns of Leeds; Thomas C. Lewis of London, Messrs. Abbott & Smith of Leeds, Messrs. Forster & Andrews of Hull and Thomas Pendlebury of Leigh, Lancashire.

Pendlebury had been devoted to the principles of Schulze throughout his career. Perhaps some words written by him in 1928 will finally convey how he regarded his art. In his book 'Matters of Interest Concerning Organs' he writes: 'Only a few hours previous to writing these notes. I was listening to the grandeur of the fundamental stops on the Schulze organ at St. Peter's Church, Hindley whilst I moved to various positions in the church. There was no getting away from its tone, it pervades into every corner of the building, and is not only heard but felt. This is mainly due to Schulze making all his basses of wood pipes; and of course, his particular form of pipe mouth construction. There is apparently a great distinction between tone that can be felt and that which is only heard. The latter can be accounted for to a great extent by our present day limited knowledge of accoustical matters.

The Pendlebury organ in Sacred Heart Catholic Church, Leigh, Lancashire. (1929).

But the tone which we feel brings our personalities into the, shall I say, the 'magnetic field' of the Spirit of God, so that even our physical bodies are affected by its influence as in no other way".

Thomas Pendlebury died on Friday December 3rd, 1933, his obituary is reported in the *Leigh Journal:*

> "The funeral took place at Westleigh, St. Paul's Church on Thursday December 7th of Mr. Thomas Pendlebury, 182 Chapel Street, Leigh. The service was conducted by the Revd. J.E. Eastwood B.A. Vicar of Westleigh; and the organ used at the service was the one Thomas Pendlebury had built.
>
> Since October Mr. Pendlebury had been a semi-invalid. Born sixty-six years ago in humble circumstances at Westleigh, his early life was spent as a miner. His musical genius, soon asserted itself, and at an early age his spare time was

Messrs. T. Boydell, Engineers & Ironfounders, Brown Street, Leigh, (circa 1920s), supplied hydraulic blowing plant for Pendlebury organs. (Photo. Wigan Record Office)

spent in attempts at organbuilding. Eventually, through his studies and experience he developed into a renowned organbuilder. Leigh and District have shown their appreciation of his genius and a large number of organs in the district have been built by him. His abilities were also recognised in the counties of Lancashire, Cheshire, Yorkshire, the Lake District and in the U.S.A. There are many testimonials to his work from clients. The outstanding features of his instruments were their excellent sound from organ pipes made of wood, and the celebrated 'violin' stop of which he was very proud. He wrote several articles on organ construction, and during his illness wrote a book for which negotiations are in progress. In 1903 he patented and invented improved mechanisms for organ windchests. His active mind was not confined to organbuilding. In 1922 he invented and patented improved safety guards for machinery and a dual control system for the motor car – he leaves a widow three daughters and two sons."

Chapter 4

James
Pendlebury
1893 - 1962

A FTER the death of Thomas Pendlebury in 1933, his eldest son James took control of the business. James Pendlebury was born on May 20th 1893. He started his apprenticeship with his father whilst still at school for one hour on Saturday mornings. This continued until the age of twelve, when he began 'half-time' work. When he was thirteen James began working full time in the workshop at Bedford Square, Leigh. He continued his education in the evenings studying geometry and architecture at Leigh Technical College.

James Pendlebury throughout his training as an organbuilder and for some time afterwards, was under a hard taskmaster in his father Thomas, who was a perfectionist. Some who knew him, thought that James was given a rather hard time.

James' younger brother, also called Thomas came into the business for a time, but later left to follow other interests.

During the 1914-18 War, James Pendlebury enlisted in the Lancashire Fusiliers. He served in France, but was later transferred to the newly formed Royal Flying Corps as a Rigger. Here he was engaged in assembling aeroplanes such as the Sopwith Camel and De Haviland 4s, which were shipped out from England and erected in France.

The Pendleburys were a talented family and following in this tradition

James Pendlebury (1893-1962).

James, like his father, had an inventive mind. On his return from active service after the war of 1914, he took an interest in the internal combustion engine and the 'wireless'. Along with his father, James built 'crystal sets' tuned on the 'cats whisker' method, later they constructed valve radios. Not surprisingly it was James who later introduced Electropneumatic actions into Pendlebury organs.

James Pendlebury continued for a time in the Bedford Square workshop, he worked alongside his father until the beginning of the 1930s. Thomas Pendlebury was as previously stated, a perfectionist, and could at times be difficult. Like almost all geniuses he had placed art before profit. His casual remark: "if we have some money in the bank, we're doing all right", must have created difficulties for James in a period of deep depression. Later in 1931 Thomas Pendlebury had been in failing health, James had made an offer to take over responsibility for the business, but to this suggestion Thomas Pendlebury would not agree. Indeed could not. His craft was a dedication of a life's work. He could not 'let go'. James also had ideas of his own, such as the introduction of electrical actions for organ mechanism; and the design of a new small instrument. This may have brought about a conflict of ideas between James and his father, together with an unwillingness to allow James to take control which brought about Thomas Pendlebury's impulsive action in James' dismissal.

Between 1931-32 James Pendlebury set up business on his own account in Brown Street, Leigh. It was a difficult time in the 30s for small businesses. James wrote many letters of introduction to churches and chapels

20 WENSLEYDALE ROAD,

LEIGH, *Lancs.*

Dec. 17th, 1932.

To Trustees Wesleyan Church Astley.

Gentlemen,

I should be grateful to you if you would be kind enough to consider the tuning of your organ. I have been responsible for your organ, along with more than 40 Church organs, and I have had a great experience of outside work such as tuning, cleaning, re-voicing and re-building.

For 26 years I have done all the outside work for my father who is now in very poor health, and dismissed me from his service on Sept. 2nd, 1932.

Yours faithfully,

JAMES PENDLEBURY
(late with Thomas Pendlebury)

ORGAN BUILDER.

This year I have built a new organ for the Centenary Methodist Church, Glazebrook, and I enclose a copy of Dr. Dixon's unsolicited report. I was responsible for the design and tone and built it (as a workman) for my father.

Right: *James Pendlebury's letter which circulated in 1932, seeking work after setting up business in Brown Street, Leigh.* **Below:** *letter headed paper (circa 1932).*

𝔓enɒlebury 𝔒rgan 𝔠o. (LEIGH) 𝔏tɒ.

Established 1898   *Successors to Thomas Pendlebury & Sons*

MANAGING DIRECTOR
J. PENDLEBURY, F.I.S.O.B.,
A.M.Inst.B.E.
DIRECTORS
S. PENDLEBURY, M.I.S.O.B.
E. E. PENDLEBURY

Works :

BROWN STREET
LEIGH, LANCASHIRE

Telephone LEIGH **369**
Station for Goods : LEIGH

𝔅uilɒers of 𝔠hurch 𝔒rgans

CLASSIFICATION "A"

Specialities : WOOD PIPES OF DIAPASON, FLUTE, AND STRING TONES
ELECTRIC, ELECTRO-PNEUMATIC AND TUBULAR PNEUMATIC ACTIONS
SILENT ELECTRIC BLOWING EQUIPMENT
RE-BUILDING, CLEANING, RE-VOICING, TUNING AND MAINTENANCE OF ORGANS BY CONTRACT

asking for their continuation of business, or in order to obtain additional work.

The break between James and his father did not however last long. On the 6th February, 1933, James received a letter from his father in which he mentioned his continuing ill-health, and asked his son James, to undertake and complete the existing commissions on his behalf, so that the maintenance of the goodwill built up over the years should remain.

An old employee of Pendlebury's, Mr. Edward Collier of Leigh, remembers the Brown Street workshop. He describes it as a single storey brick building. People travelling from Leigh Station by train to Liverpool obtained a good view of the building with its large letters proudly announcing PENDLEBURY ORGAN COMPANY. Internally the workshop comprised two sections the front portion having a fairly large wooden floor on which was erected a small office. The remaining section had either a stone or concrete floor, used for erecting organs and for storage. There were racks for timber, pipes and fittings. Heating was provided from a coke boiler situated at the rear of the building at a low level. Mr. Collier remembers that this was subject to flooding from time to time, due to its close proximity with the Leigh Bridgewater Canal. The woodworking

Pendlebury Organ Works, Brown Street, Leigh. Circa 1933. (Photo. Wigan Record Office)

machinery comprised of a fairly large circular saw used for quickly converting timber into working sections, a small circular saw, a jig saw, planing machine and a drilling machine set on an iron stand in the centre of the shop; also one or two work benches situated in the front section of the workshop. All the machinery was belt driven from an overhead line-shaft, a method of power that today would have been condemned.

The tonal conception of the Pendlebury organ did not change under James. Indeed, why should it? The harmonic development of its chorus was more mature and colourful than those being produced by other provincial builders. The rich bass notes of the Pedal organ and the lower octaves on the manuals (keyboards) were obtained by the use of wooden pipes of almost square sections and to the same scale as those used by his father Thomas. The quality of tone in the trebles had a clear bright clarity, but most important, every stop blended with its neighbour. The whole ensemble producing solo voices, a variety of choruses at various levels and in the full organ a solidity which gave a colourful chorus touched with a hint of grandeur. These qualities are the 'hallmark' of the Pendlebury instrument.

The tonal schemes of James Pendlebury rarely, if ever, included a 'mixture' stop. On occasion there does appear a mutation rank (a stop which sounds at a pitch other than that of unison or one of its octaves) sounding the Twelfth harmonic, but the choruses did not develop beyond this. James remained firmly entrenched in the Pendlebury claim that enough harmonics were introduced into the structure of their Diapason or main chorus at 8 ft., 4 ft., and 2 ft. pitches, that there were abundant overtones, mixtures were not required. This seems strange when we consider Thomas Pendlebury's fine achievement in chorus work, with the introduction of his first Mixture stop and a beautifully voiced 16 ft. reed, Corno di Bassetto, on the Swell organ at St. Paul's Parish Church, Westleigh.

Continuing in the traditions of the firm, James built a number of two-manual-three model instruments, an innovation of his father's. An excellent example of this style may still be seen in the Methodist Church, Glazebrook, near Warrington. This instrument appears to have been built during the transitional period in the firms history. The opening programme for 1932 states – 'built by James Pendlebury, Bedford Square, Leigh'.

The *Leigh Journal* 1909 gives an eye witness account of the opening of Glazebrook Chapel:

"It was a great day in the history of this rural farming community.
Almost the whole of the inhabitants had been absorbed in the work.

That day I rode my bicycle through the fields in the direction of Glazebrook; feeling the exhilarating touch of a glorious winters' day. The air was clear and sharp, but a brisk ride of six-and-a-half miles warmed my body. At 3.30 p.m. in the distance a crowd of some three hundred people were singing lustily "All People that on Earth do dwell" to the rousing tune 'Montgomery'. It was an ideal winter scene, glorious country covered with frost stretching for miles on either side. There was a company of happy faces and many vigorous handshakes. The Revd. W. Judson gave a short address, a Golden Key was presented to Miss Hartley of Southport who opened the chapel door".

The building comprising Chapel and Sunday School is built of Ruabon Brick & Tile to a design by the Architect Everard W. Leeson, 49 Princess Street, Manchester: builder Messrs. Brew Bros. of Cadishead. Total cost of the building £1,367.00.

In 1932 the Chapel Committee having no doubt cleared many outstanding debts asked James Pendlebury to build their organ. This he carried out on the two-manual-three system of Thomas Pendlebury. It is positioned in a chamber on the north wall, rather than in the more usual position in the choir at the front. But here James seized an opportunity to set out the instrument on a wide horizontal plane, in four separate sections, two of which are enclosed e.g. the Swell and part of the Great or main section. The instrument tonally is a great success, and in spite of its apparent limitations it copes extremely well over a wide spectrum. It is thoroughly musical, with a good deal of character and colour in its voicing. The materials from which it is built are of the highest quality with timber free from defects. The opening recital was given by Dr. J.H. Reginald-Dixon. Organist of Lancaster Catholic Cathedral, who later expressed his appreciation of Pendlebury's work.

J.H. Reginald Dixon, D.Mus., F.R.C.O.

Meadowside, Lancaster.
June 20th, 1932.

To James Pendlebury, Esq., Leigh.

Dear Mr. Pendlebury,

I have just come away from trying over the new organ you have built for the Primitive Methodist Chapel at Glazebrook, and it gives me much pleasure to state my impressions of the instrument.

The casework strikes one as being well in keeping with the general surroundings, and the design is both interesting and effective. The touch of the keys is nice and light, and the action is quick and responsive. The tonal scheme includes the enclosure of three of the stops of the Great Organ, and this vastly increases the resources of the organ in expressive playing. The wood string and Diapason basses, invariably a distinguishing feature of the Pendlebury organs, are again in evidence and are beautifully voiced. From the softest stop right up to the full organ the tone of the organ is even, smooth and delightfully mellow. There is no trace of harshness anywhere. The work inside the organ has been done as carefully as that on the outside, and it reflects the greatest credit on you who built it, thereby carrying on the sound traditions with which your father's name has long been associated. Please accept my very sincere congratulations on the success you have achieved.

Yours faithfully,

J.H. Reginald Dixon

D.Mus., F.R.C.O., Organist, The Cathedral, Lancaster.

Organ Recital by Dr. J.H. Reginald-Dixon, D.Mus., F.R.C.O.

Prelude & Fugue in E Flat	J.S. Bach
A Song of Sunshine	Hollins
Serenade	Schubert
The Londonderry Air arr	J.A. Meale
Part Song "Hymn to Music"	Dudley Buck
Largo	G.F. Handel
The Clock is Playing	Pierre Blaauw
Intermezzo	F. Lehar
Sonata No. 1	Mendelssohn
Air. "Let the Bright Seraphim"	G.F. Handel
Stanchen	Heykens
The Night Patrol	Jean Martell
a) A Glazebrooke Melody	
b) Improvisation on Well Known Tunes	J.H. Reginald-Dixon
Suite "In India"	R.N. Sloughton

The Grove of Palms. By the Ganges.

Indian Dance at Delhi. A Mysterious Incantation.

In the Palace of the Rajah.

However like all sons James Pendlebury wished to branch out with some development of his own. In 1934 he designed an instrument for the small church or chapel, and strictly for accompaniment. This instrument was known as the 'Enchantona'. It was really an improved development of his father's two-manual-three instrument. There was a standard specification; the cost depending upon the type of mechanism used was £395-0-0 for pneumatic action and £425-0-0 for electrical action. The casework was of English Oak or Pitch Pine and the console of polished oak or mahogany. All the pipework was enclosed including the pedal section, and the lower keyboard was designated Choir Organ, rather than its usual title of Great or main organ.

A leaflet promoting the 'Enchantona' was published by James Pendlebury:

> In introducing the 'Enchantona' Organ to the Musical Public we have endeavoured to supply the need for a really good sound Musical Instrument at a reasonable cost. It will support a congregation of 250/300 people and has interesting possibilities as a Solo Organ, with a little modification in its voicing it would make an admirable Organ for a private Music Room. Our aim has been to produce an organ capable of the maximum possibilities under the limitations of price.
>
> It is not an extension organ. We have never countenanced the use of manual (keyboard) extension systems, or ranks of pipes used over and over again in order to obtain different effects. Rows of stopkeys may look very impressive, but they do not make music.
>
> The lower manual (keyboard) is purely for accompaniment with two

The Two-Manual-Three Model Organ in Glazebrook Methodist Church, near Warrington. (Photo. Wigan Record Office)

ranks of pipes Salicional and Celeste. These pipes are enclosed in a separate swell box. On the Swell manual (Upper Keyboard) there is a variety of Solo stops but they will all blend perfectly, thus making a chorus of solid dignified tone for congregational support. Included is the famous Pendlebury 'Violin Diapason' which forms the foundation of this section and is one of our Special Wood Stops. It is voiced with keen string tone, used with the Tremulant a very beautiful 'cello' effect is obtained in the lower octaves. Eminent Musical Authorities have declared 'it is an organ in itself'.

The Pendlebury 'Enchantona' is made of the best possible materials and by craftsmen who have trained from boyhood in the profession of Organbuilding. Every piece of timber is carefully scrutinized, and should a fault be found even in a partly machined piece, however advanced the process, the whole piece finds its way to the boiler fire. All materials, including the metal pipes (which we do not make ourselves) are of the highest quality. We are proud of our workmanship and we cordially invite anyone to visit us.

All our instruments are erected and tried before leaving the workshop. Thus they are built in atmospheric conditions similar to the buildings in which they are to stand. Never in the history of the firm have we failed to have an instrument completed by the opening date, and never has an 'Opening Programme' been marred by a note cyphering. Our special low pressure pneumatic-action is too well known to elaborate upon it here, we have actions over thirty-years old still functioning with the same silence and reliability as when first built. We have now evolved an Electro-Pneu-

James Pendlebury's 'Enchantona' instrument. All Saints Church, Leigh.

matic Action which we have found extremely reliable.

The present head of the firm has over thirty years practical experience and his advice is freely at the disposal of prospective purchasers. We hope to continue to merit the trust reposed in us for many years by satisfied clients.

Pendlebury Organ Works, Leigh.

One of these 'Enchantonas' may be found still giving satisfactory service in All Saint's Church, Manchester Road, Leigh. It is built to the standards outlined in James Pendlebury's leaflet.

James' son and daughter, Stanley and Edna were involved in the business, and as the letterheads of the Firm show became co- directors. Edna was also Company Secretary. The 1939-45 War created many difficulties in the organbuilding trade, both in supply of materials and in the availability of trained organbuilders. In those difficult years it was not unknown for Miss Edna Pendlebury to frequently don a boiler suit and assist in cleaning and repairs of many instruments.

For a short time during the War, the Pendlebury Organ Company carried out some war work for a local engineering firm manufacturing Air-Raid Shelter Filters. These would have provided clean-air in the event of gas warfare.

In the footsteps of his father, James took over the care of the famous Schulze organ in St. Peter's Church, Hindley, which at this period was powered by a hydraulic engine. The Pendlebury firm had based their tonal designs in the style of this great artist, and were proud of their long association with the instrument. A well known local musician Mr. William Rigby of Hindley Green, remembers James maintaining the instrument at St. Peter's. 'Bill' as he likes to be known was then assistant organist at St. Peter's, Hindley, and had also been organist at a number of churches and chapels in the district.

'Bill' Rigby in the 1930's and during the war years took over the music shop of T. Royle, 39 Market Street, Hindley, where he sold sheet music and musical instruments. "If it played a tune, I sold it" he remarks. 'Bill' now in his eighties has a store of musical anecdotes. He recalls the occasional troubles with the water engine at St. Peter's Church, which would over rotate when full choruses were not in use. He and James Pendlebury worked out a counter-weight system to combat this problem; using piano wires from 'Bills' music shop. When he was assistant at St. Peter's, the organ console in those days was placed between the two west end organ cases (in the position Edmund Schulze left it in 1873). During Harvest Festivals bunches of grapes

76

were hung from the corners of the casework. 'Bill' says, "I had a passion for green grapes, and during the Sermon I tried one, and another, and – when the sermon ended – so had the grapes". At subsequent 'Harvests' there were no more grapes hung on the organ case.

During his career as a local organist 'Bill' Rigby received many requests to play favourite melodies; one such request from a friend, who, choosing the type of music to be played at her demise, asked for "I've Got a Lovely Bunch of Coconuts" as she was taken out of church. In those days there was not the flexibility in church music that we enjoy today. But says 'Bill'. I altered the timing a little, did a bit of improvising. There were a few raised eyebrows, and the Vicar was a little suspicious, but I got away with it". William 'Bill' Rigby, also played the cinema organs for the silent screen, at the Palace Cinema, Hindley and the Pavillion Picture House, Wigan (The latter stood on the site now occupied by Wigan baths). These were the early Orchestrion Organs built by the well known firm of J.W. Jardine & Co., Manchester.

William 'Bill' Rigby at the console of the Schulze organ in St. Peter's Church, Hindley, Lancashire. (Photo. Wigan Record Office).

During his career James Pendlebury had restored or rebuilt some of his father's instruments. One of the last to be rebuilt by him was the 1903 instrument in Atherton Baptist Church. This instrument, apart from regular tuning had required no attention to its action since its installation.

In 1947 the church authorities consulted Thomas Pendlebury's successors The Pendlebury Organ Company, Leigh. The directors being the son, grandson, and grand-daughter respectively. It was decided that the 1903 instrument which Mr. Miles Burrows of Atherton, the original donor had commissioned Thomas Pendlebury to build should be modernized and enlarged in memory of him and his wife.

James Pendlebury proposed a scheme which left the original specification of its creator intact but augmented and rendered more flexible by certain additions. James made the following modifications. A new detached stopkey console placed centrally in front of the choir stalls. Made of oak and wax finished, the action was James' own electro-pneumatic system, with electrical relays placed in dust-proof glass cases. The tonal additions made at this period were five new stops to the Swell organ (upper keyboard) two stops to the Great organ (middle keyboard) and a string toned stop to the Choir organ (lower keyboard) together with some additional couplers which enabled the various keyboards to be played in unison or in octaves. Here was the work of Father, Son and Grandson (Stanley).

The instrument was re-opened on November 20th, 1948, with a recital given by Mr. Harold Dawber F.R.C.O. University Organist (Manchester) and Professor of Organ at the Royal Manchester College of Music.

It is said that organbuilding runs in families. And present at the opening of this instrument were four generations of Pendlebury's: Mrs. M.H. Pendlebury, sen., widow of Thomas Pendlebury; Mr. & Mrs. James Pendlebury and their daughter, Miss Edna Pendlebury; Mr. & Mrs. Stanley Pendlebury and their infant daughter, Sandra Vivian (aged nine weeks). The last named seemed to enjoy the proceedings until the minister's address, when she audibly expressed her disapproval.

The Atherton Baptist Church has suffered from structural problems for many years due to mining subsidence within the area. In 1986-87 this fine building was demolished and a smaller more modern structure built on the site at a safer position. Thomas Pendlebury's instrument was removed by another company of organbuilders.

In 1952 the Pendlebury firm transferred its business to Blackpool. James had been living in the area for some time, he therefore no doubt felt that this new venture was the wise course to follow, that it would open a new area for business.

Soon after the Firm moved to Blackpool, James produced another brochure outlining the Firm's history and service to the musical public. A brief resumé of the business was given from 1898, that of a family concern, and was inaugurated into a Limited Company.

The various branches and type of work carried out are described, with voicing of the pipes being carried out by a member of the family. The directors being all working craftsmen. Advice is included on the purchase of new organs. Instruments built upon the extension system were frowned upon at this period by the Pendlebury Company. It was stressed that in an organ built by the company every stop is composed of a complete rank of pipes. Advice is also included on the choice and type of action to be employed in the instrument they wish to purchase. Mention is also made that Pendlebury's first pneumatic action to the keyboards was designed in 1906 and is still working (1952) without any repairs being carried out. Further advice is included regarding rebuilding existing instruments, cleanings and overhauling, tuning contacts and organ blowers etc.

Between 1933-1961 James Pendlebury built some fifteen organs and carried out rebuilding to many others. He is remembered by many who knew him, especially Mr. Arthur Scholes of Leigh and Mrs. Betty Pendlebury (daugthers-in-law) as a quiet kindly man possessing a great sense of humour.

James Pendlebury FISOB. A.M.Inst.B.E. died on March 17th, 1962, aged 68 years and is buried in Thornton churchyard.

Chapter 5

Stanley Pendlebury 1919 - 1988

THE family tradition was continued with Stanley Pendlebury; James' son and grandson of the founder Thomas Pendlebury. Stanley was born on September 21st, 1919. Followed some two years later by a sister Edna.

Mr. Arthur Scholes, now living in Manchester Road, Leigh was a school friend of Stanley Pendlebury. As children they attended Bedford Wesleyan School, Leigh. Arthur remembers Stanley as having a generous nature, particularly with his possessions. He remembers sharing a scooter made by Stanley's father James. "It was painted dark red, and rather unusual, as it had a sort of pedal or lever so that once momentum was started by a push this could be continued by working the pedal, which acted as a drive. We had lots of fun riding up and down Holden Road, Leigh". Without doubt this pedal movement was derived from an organ mechanism, the idea of James Pendlebury.

From being very young Stanley Pendlebury 'helped' his father and grandfather at the organ works in Bedford Square, Leigh. He soon learned to be useful. At the age of fourteen Stanley began working full-time as an organbuilders apprentice. His wages at this period in 1932 were five shillings per week (25p). This sum was later increased to twelve shillings and sixpence per week (62p).

In later years Stanley worked alongside his father in the 'new' workshop in Brown Street, Leigh. The instruments they produced at this period were

Stanley Pendlebury (1919-1988).

in the style of the late Thomas Pendlebury with the same tonal quality. The choruses were still devoid of any 'mixturework' or 'mutations'. Nevertheless Stanley learned his craft well. He was a natural. He once told the author: "I never wished to do anything else but build pipe organs."

The hostilities of the 1939-45 war put an end to organbuilding for Stanley Pendlebury. During this period he saw service in the Royal Army Ordnance Corps., later becoming a founder member of the newly formed Royal Electrical & Mechanical Engineers. He served in North Africa, Italy and Austria as a sergeant fitter. His knowledge of electrical actions and mechanical movements proved invaluable at this time. Stanley was also mentioned in despatches and awarded the twin Oak Leaves.

Whilst on active service in this country, Stanley Pendlebury met Miss Betty Amor. Later they married and set up home in Leigh. Finally moving to Cleveleys when the firm transferred its business. The family of Stanley and Betty Pendlebury consisted of two daughters Sandra Vivian and Jean.

After the war Stanley Pendlebury returned to civilian life as co-director of the firm with his father.

As the century moved towards the 1950s, styles in organbuilding were changing, the period known as the 'Organ Reform Movement' was heralded in with the design for a large concert organ at the Royal Festival Hall, London. So, too, was it time for change for Pendleburys. James Pendlebury retired from business life. The Company moved from Layton Road, Blackpool and under Stanley moved into a new modern workshop at Dorset Avenue, Thornton-Cleveleys.

Thomas Pendlebury, founder of the firm had been a progressive, both in his tonal skills and inventive mechanisms. Stanley, his grandson was a 'chip off the old block', and perhaps the most progressive. He realized too, that the firm had to move with the musical trends of the time, even if his grandfather might not have totally approved.

The author first made his acquaintance with Stanley Pendlebury early in the 1960s, and a friendship developed which lasted for some twenty-six years. During this time a number of instruments were built and restored in which the author acted as adviser. It was over this period of time that Stanley Pendlebury's open and generous nature revealed itself as remembered by his school pal Arthur Scholes. Stanley never tired of talking about organbuilding and organ design and his knowledge was freely shared with all who showed interest in a subject which was dear to his heart.

The 1950s and early 60s was a period which saw the introduction of the caseless organ, or as it was sometimes referred to as 'a functional pipe display'. These designs were really off-shoots of the pipe display at the Royal Festival Hall, but without the latters aesthetic qualities. The Pendlebury Organ Company at this period took a middle course. Following the trends of the period they produced both caseless instruments and partial casework i.e. display pipes and panels.

Stanley Pendlebury now took the opportunity of following what both his grandfather and father had done before him. He produced something of his own. This was a small but very versatile organ, capable of leading fairly large congregations and on which some recital work was possible. It was built upon the extension or duplication system (A method in which ranks of pipes are extended beyond their normal compass, or the same ranks are used on another keyboard). This method enables stops of different pitches to be obtained from a single rank of pipes, or the same rank to be used on another keyboard at a different pitch. This instrument was called the 'THORNTON'. Its tonal design was based on the blending of stops one with another in the Pendlebury tradition; but now there was included a 'mixture' and 'mutation' ranks. The action was electro-pneumatic; the consoles were of the stop-key type and either attached or detached as suited the situation.

Stanley Pendlebury published a leaflet describing the merits of his design, this was based on three ranks of pipes spread over two manuals and pedals. In this design couplers were not required. The stops on the Swell organ (upper manual) which would be useful on the Great organ (lower manual) are independently placed on this keyboard, so that it is possible to obtain the full organ effect on this lower manual. There is also a wide range of stops on the Pedal organ with the advantage that they may be used without their manual extension, thus enabling solo passages to be performed on the pedal department. These instruments are erected in a very short time and built of high quality materials and carry the firm's twenty five year guarantee. The 'Thornton' Organ specification comprised of three ranks of pipes from which the following stops were obtained:

Great Organ

Double Open Diapason (Ten.C.)	16'
Open Diapason	8'
Stopped Diapason	8'
Salicional	8'
Principal	4'
Flute	4'
Twelfth	$2^2/3$'

Pedal Organ

Bourdon	16'
Open Diapason	8'
Salicional	8'
Bass Flute	8'
Principal	4'
Flute	4'

Swell Organ

Contra Salicional (Ten.C.)	16'
Stopped Diapason	8'
Salicional	8'
Salicet	4'
Flute	4'
Piccolo	2'
Tremulant (General)	

The 'Thornton' instrument proved to be very popular and other models were built with a 73 note reed unit, the pipes made of zinc and unplaned organ metal. This unit provided these instruments with a Harmonic Trumpet on both keyboards and a Trombone and Clarion on the pedal organ. Later a three rank mixture was included. All instruments built by Pendlebury now contained stops providing various pitches of the harmonic scale. This tonal development was a distinct advance from that of his father and grandfather, but maintaining the Pendlebury tradition in the use of good materials. When many organbuilding firms were purchasing ready made organ consoles and casework panels made from veneered boarding, the Pendlebury Organ Company continued to make consoles and other sections in their workshop from solid oak or other hardwoods.

On one occasion the author was engaged on a commission where cash was in short supply, parts of the existing organ were to be re- used including the rather noisy electrical blower. On paying a regular evening visit to see how the job was progressing he found a small new blowing unit on site. The old blowing plant had been discreetly removed and the new blower was a gift from the Pendlebury Organ Company.

Some of the instruments in which the author was engaged as adviser with Stanley Pendlebury were as follows:

> St. John's Catholic Church, Wigan. (New Thornton Organ with reed unit).
> Sacred Heart Catholic Church, Hindley Green, Wigan. (Thornton Organ with re-used pipework).
> Christ's Church, Parish Church, Ince-in-Makerfield, Wigan. (Rebuild of Hill Organ).
> St. Mary's, Parish Church, Ince-in-Makerfield, Wigan. (Rebuild of Co-nacher organ).
> St. Nathanial's Parish Church, Platt Bridge, Wigan. (Rebuild of Jardine organ).
> St. Mary's Parish Church, Gisburn, Yorkshire. (Restoration of Lewis organ).
> St. George's Parish Church, Atherton. Manchester (Rebuild).
> St. Matthew's Catholic Church, Queens Drive, Liverpool. (New Organ).
> St. Paul's U.R. Church, Wigan. (New Organ).
> St. Peter's Parish Church, Hindley. (Part restoration of Schulze organ. 1873).
> St. Oswald's Catholic Church, Ashton-in-Makerfield. (Restoration of Stalhuth organ. Aachen).

Many of the instruments built or restored by Stanley Pendlebury were opened by organists of national and international fame. When engaged on the restoration of the famous Schulze instrument in St. Peter's Church, Hindley, Stanley followed his grandfather in care of this instrument restoring

The movable three manual console fitted to the Schulze organ at St. Peter's Church, Hindley, Lancashire.

two sections and adding a new three manual detached drawstop console placed on a movable platform . The console is of English Oak with raised and fielded panels finished with carved dentils, the stop jambs, music desk and pedal sharps are of Indian Rosewood. The opening recital was given by the international concert organist Gillian Weir.

Stanley Pendlebury was an accomplished musician. When he was quite small his first music lessons were given by a lady living in Wensleydale Road, Leigh. Stanley knew her as 'Aunty Mary', although she was not related to the Pendleburys. However, these lessons did not last very long, Stanley had other ideas. On one occasion when he was about fourteen years old, Stanley arrived home with a piece of music saying: "Look, please don't laugh at me, I'm going to teach myself to play the piano". Why should he not? All the members of the Pendlebury family were talented in various ways. The founder of the firm was a self taught organbuilder and tuner. James Pendlebury also had an inventive mind, and had introduced their first electric action in the organ at All Saints Parish Church, Manchester Road, Leigh. It was natural that the grandson should follow the family trend. Betty Pendlebury recalls Stanley's playing ability in earlier years: "He seemed to have a natural gift, his greatest

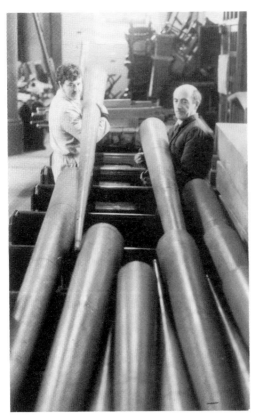

Stanley Pendlebury (right) refitting the 16 ft. Posaune pipes in St. Peter's Church, Hindley, Lancashire.

pleasure was to extemporise. When we first met in our early twenties there was a piano at my home and the first piece of music Stan ever played for me was Cavelleria Rusticana (Mascagni). It was played with such feeling and sensitivity and remains a treasured memory".

On completion of an organ Stanley Pendlebury would find an opportunity to be alone and extemporise at some length, and on one occasion the author was fortunate enough to be around during one of Stan's quiet half-hours. It was a great pleasure to sit and listen to him.

The workshop at Dorset Avenue, Cleveleys was a well lighted airy building, equipped with modern woodworking machinery, workbenches and space for erecting instruments and storage of timber. There was also a small office, on the wall of which was a map dotted with many coloured pins, showing the areas where work was in progress or where tuning contracts were held. And on the window ledge in the centre of the office a framed photograph of Thomas Pendlebury.

Other commissions carried out under Stanley Pendlebury's directorship of the company:

> Gidlow Methodist Church, Wigan.
> Christ's Parish Church, Fulwood.
> Bispham Parish Church, Blackpool.

St. Mark's Parish Church, Barrow-in-Furness.
Stockton Heath Methodist Church.
Poulton le Fylde Methodist Church.
Springfield Methodist Church, Blackpool.
St. Mary's Parish Chuch, Blackpool.
St. Nicholas Parish Church, Blackpool.
Rawcliffe Methodist Church, Fylde.
Victoria Congregational Church, Blackpool.
The Grammar School, Wigan.
Middleton Parish Church, Manchester.
Eccleston Methodist Church, St. Helens.
Bolton Parish Church.
Trinity United Reform Church, Wigan.

The above list is by no means complete. These instruments had a different tonal structure from the Pendlebury organs of earlier years with well developed choruses on all manuals and bright modern reedwork or orchestral colouring. But the traditions of the past were not forogotten; the pedal department still retained its rich string bass quality, flutes were as clear and pure as in the founder's day, and the completed instruments were full of 'life'. In fact one did not tire of exploring their possibilities. A client once asked Stanley Pendlebury which was the finest organ he had built? He replied: "The best organ we build will be our next one".

In 1974 an important rebuilding with certain modifications was carried out on the 1894 E.F. Walcker organ at The Drive Methodist Church, St. Annes-on-Sea. Here the historical pipework was preserved and fortunately was so scaled as to lend itself to the modifications carried out by the firm. This was followed some four years later by another historical restoration to the instrument in St. Thomas's Catholic Church, Claughton, Lancashire. An instrument of 1859 vintage built by J.C. Bishop a well known London organbuilder. This beautiful instrument was preserved with its mahogany casework, together with the short pedalboard and Tenor.C. Swell organ, both the organ and church are worth a visit situated in delightful countryside. The latter restorations were carried out with the advice of Dr. Gerald Sumner of Preston.

Stanley Pendlebury was a progressive, completely devoted to his craft. He restored or rebuilt and produced more new instruments than either his father or grandfather. During the 1980s the firm reverted back to its roots as The Thomas Pendlebury Organ Company.

One of the last instruments on which Stanley Pendlebury was engaged was for the new United Reform Church, Wigan. The author was engaged as advisor. This instrument was completed and the opening recital given by the international concert organist Jennifer Bate on November 29th, 1980. It is interesting to compare the specification with those produced in the earlier years of the firm.

Great Organ		Swell Organ	
Open Diapason	8'	Rhor Flote	8'
Stopped Diapason	8'	Salicional	8'
Octave	4'	Spitz Flote	4'
Fifteenth	2'	Gemshorn	2'
Mixture 19:22:26	3rks	Larigot	$1^1/3$'
Pedal Organ		Trumpet	8'
Sub Bass	16'	Tremulant	
Bass Flote	8'	**Couplers.**	
Principal	8'	Swell to Great	
Choral Bass	4'	Swell to Pedal	
Fifteenth	4'	Great to Pedal	
Bassoon	16'		

This instrument was designed to accompany both a traditional and modern liturgy and also to be capable of performing a wide selection of organ repertoire for recital use.

It was erected in a modern building, the pipework and its casework is positioned on the main tie-beams of the roof truss. The console placed upon a movable platform which is very useful in recital work.

Opening programme played by International concert Organist Jennifer Bate:

Sonata No. I in F minor (i) Allegro moderato e maestoso (ii) Adagio (iii) Andante - Recitativo (iv) Allegro assai vivace	Felix Mendelssohn
Sketch No. 4 in D Flat	Robert Schumann
Toccata, Adagio and Fugue in C.	J.S. Bach
Sonata No. 4 in E minor (i) Adagio - Vivace (ii) Andante (iii) Un poco allegro	J.S. Bach
Variations on "King Jesus hath a garden"	Flor Peeters
Pastorale	Louis Vierne

AN ENGLISH ORGAN

We have been so inundated by Continental ideas on organ tone during the past decade or so that we decided to take a broad view and consider the merits of the early English organ builders. This is not to say that no good has come across the Channel but why not have the best of both worlds and retain our individuality at the same time?

This then was our aim in designing the organ. We have the full, smooth non-chiffing Diapason chorus topped by a high-pitched Mixture which although ample for full organ, can be used with the softer combinations.

You like the 'Chiff'? So do we, and it will be found on the ranks which suit this characteristic.

Open tip voicing? Yes, again where suitable.

Nicking? Not on some ranks but just enough where necessary.

Comments we have had to date are Dignified, Crisp, Rich, Clear, Pure Toned, Brilliant.

We believe it sets a new trend and it's ENGLISH.

PENDLEBURY

ORGAN COMPANY

Dorset Avenue, Cleveleys, Lancs.

Man. Director
(and voicer):
S. Pendlebury, F.I.S.O.B.

Telephone: Cleveleys 2974   Est. 1898

ST. MATTHEW'S R.C. CHURCH QUEEN'S DRIVE, LIVERPOOL

The new organ is divided across the West gallery with a centrally placed detached drawstop console of mahogany.

GREAT

Open Diapason	...	8	61
Stopped Diapason	...	8	61
Dolce	... ...	8	61
Octave	... ...	4	61
Twelfth	...	$2\frac{2}{3}$	61
Fifteenth	... ...	2	16
Mixture 26.29.36	3 ranks		183

SWELL

Quintaton	... ...	8	61
Gemshorn	...	4	61
Köppel Flute	...	4	61
Hornlein	... ...	2	61
Tertian 17.19	2 ranks		122
Fagott	...	16	61

PEDAL

Subbass	... ...	16	30
Flute Bass (ext)	...	8	12
Octave	...	8	30
Fifteenth (ext)	...	4	12
Dulzian	...	8	30

Great to Pedal
Swell to Pedal
Swell to Great

Action: El/pneumatic to slider soundboards and basses of unit ranks. Direct electric to remainder of unit chests. Swell action mechanical.

4 thumb and toe pistons to Great and Pedal
4 thumb and toe pistons to Swell
1 thumb and toe piston to Great to Pedal
1 thumb and toe piston to Swell to Great
Selectors are provided.
3 reservoirs of traditional design.
Casework and the bulk of the interior timber is yellow pine.
Wind pressures:
  Manuals: $2\frac{1}{2}$ in.
  Pedals: $2\frac{3}{4}$ in.

The Organ: Vol LII. 1972.

Two movements from Symphony I   Charles M. Widor
(i) Intermezzo
(ii) Marche Pontificale

The above programme makes an interesting comparison with those played in earlier years, and reflects the changing tastes of the musical public. Under Stanley Pendlebury's directorship the firm received high praise for the quality of their instruments from organists of national and international repute. There were also many press reports including full page coverage of the firm's achievements but throughout their history they chose to remain a small personal family business. Examples of their craftsmanship may be found throughout the United Kingdom, their fame had also spread beyond our shores.

In the early 1980s due to increasing rheumatoid arthritis from which Stanley had suffered for some time, it was decided that the business should be sold. It is fitting therefore that this would should end by allowing Thomas

Organ casework Trinity United Reform Church, Wigan.

THE THORNTON ORGAN
Traditional Design

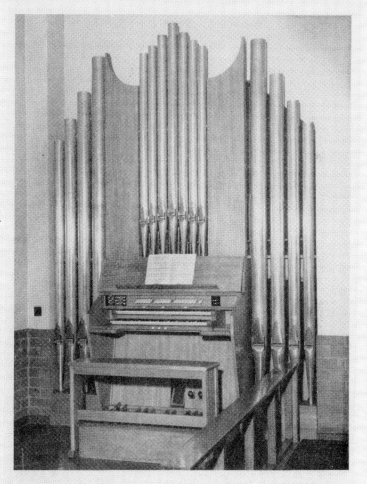

THE PENDLEBURY ORGAN COMPANY LIMITED
DORSET AVENUE · CLEVELEYS · BLACKPOOL · LANCASHIRE · ENGLAND

Gidlow Methodist Church, Wigan.

Pendlebury's grandson to speak on behalf of his father and grandfather, here are Stanley Pendlebury's sentiments of their lives devoted to their art:

"The true organ is a mass of contradiction, perfect and yet full of imperfections. Perfect in that it is an example to man of how varying characters can blend together in harmony. The pipes represent the human race, from the delicate and subdued through a vast range to the strident and assertive and yet, when under the control of the master, all blend in a harmonious whole. And yet it is imperfect because it is made by man who, notwithstanding his striving for perfection, cannot voice or tune every pipe to scientific uniformity. It is this lack of uniformity, just as in man, that brings the two so closely together and imparts the power of appealing to more than the conscious mind".

Stanley Pendlebury died on July 17th, 1988, aged 68 years and with his death the Pendlebury dynasty of Lancashire organbuilders came to its close.

GENEALOGY

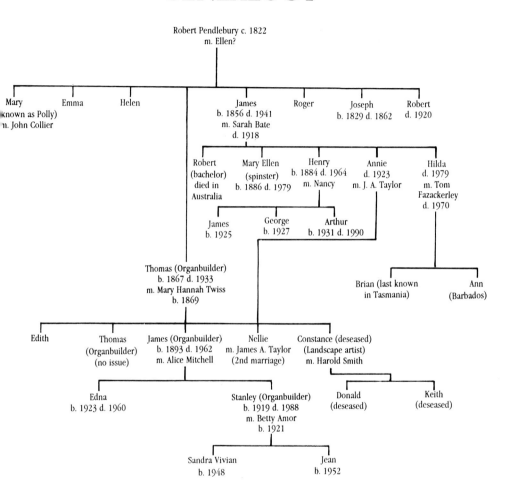

Robert Pendlebury c. 1822
m. Ellen?

Mary (known as Polly) m. John Collier — Emma — Helen — James b. 1856 d. 1941 m. Sarah Bate d. 1918 — Roger — Joseph b. 1829 d. 1862 — Robert d. 1920

Robert (bachelor) died in Australia — Mary Ellen (spinster) b. 1886 d. 1979 — Henry b. 1884 d. 1964 m. Nancy — Annie d. 1923 m. J. A. Taylor — Hilda d. 1979 m. Tom Fazackerley d. 1970

James b. 1925 — George b. 1927 — Arthur b. 1931 d. 1990

Thomas (Organbuilder) b. 1867 d. 1933 m. Mary Hannah Twiss b. 1869

Brian (last known in Tasmania) — Ann (Barbados)

Edith — Thomas (Organbuilder) (no issue) — James (Organbuilder) b. 1893 d. 1962 m. Alice Mitchell — Nellie m. James A. Taylor (2nd marriage) — Constance (deseased) (Landscape artist) m. Harold Smith

Edna b. 1923 d. 1960 — Stanley (Organbuilder) b. 1919 d. 1988 m. Betty Amor b. 1921 — Donald (deseased) — Keith (deseased)

Sandra Vivian b. 1948 — Jean b. 1952

SUBSCRIBERS

William Rigby of Hindley Green, Wigan. Organist at various local churches and ex-theatre organist of the silent screen.

British Gas plc North Western (Bolton).

Dobson Park Industries plc, Ince, Wigan.

W. Neville Blakey, Brierfield, Nelson, Lancashire.

Douglas Fairhurst, Atherton & Oxford.

Messrs. Harrison & Harrison, Organbuilders, Durham.

Messrs. J.W. Walker & Sons Ltd., Organbuilders, Brandon, Suffolk.

Professor Herbert Winterbottom D.Mus. Ph.D. L.R.A.M. F.R.S.A., Stockport, Cheshire.

Together with three generous subscribers who wish to remain anonymous.

Ashcroft H. of Fearnhead, Warrington.

Battersby K. of Leigh. (Great-nephew of Thomas Pendlebury)

Battersby R. of Leigh. (Great-nephew of Thomas Pendlebury)

Boardman P. of Atherton.

Brodie S. (nee Pendlebury) & Brodie G.

Brown K. of Leigh.

Cayton P.N. of Lowton, Warrington.

Coates R. of Glazebrook, Warrington.

Cooke G.A. of Winstanley, Wigan.

Cotterill A.C. (Mrs) of Swinton, Manchester.

Edwards L. (Mrs) of Lancaster.

Elliott J. (Ms) of Nelson.

Fell T. of Atherton.

Finch R.N. & E.S. of Lowton, Warrington.

Giles C.L. of Leigh.

Harrison J.A. of Heaton, Bolton.

Hilton, S. of Longshaw, Billinge, Wigan.

Latham J. of Leigh.

SUBSCRIBERS (cont.)

Marsh R. (Mrs) of Lichfield, Staffs. (Great-niece of Thomas
     Pendlebury)

Martin E. (Mrs) of Leigh.

Mason J.E. of Bolton (Organbuilder).

Mitchell P.K. of Burnley.

Neal D. of Leigh.

Pendlebury G. of Leigh.

Pendlebury J. of Mirfield, West Yorkshire.

Platt A. of Swinton, Manchester.

Price E. of Morecambe.

Tomlinson P. Organist Burnley Parish Church.

Topham M.M. of Middleton, Manchester.

Welsby N. (Mrs) of Leigh. (Niece of Thomas Pendlebury)

Whitehead I. (Mrs) of Swinton, Manchester. (Great-niece of
     Thomas Pendlebury).

Wigan MBC Leisure Services.

Winstanley J. (Mrs) of Leigh. (Great-niece of Thomas Pendlebury)

S.M. Woodward (Mrs) of Hindley Green, Wigan.

Wressell C.M. (Mrs) of Chester. (Grand-daughter of Thomas
     Pendlebury)

REFERENCES

Lecture notes - Leigh Historical Society (1910). W.D. Pink, JP. F.R.M.S.

The *Leigh Journal*. 1909, 1914, 1933.

The *Leigh Chronicle*. 1900, 1902, 1903, 1909, 1914.

Musical Opinion. 1908, 1909, 1959, 1980.

The Art of Organbuilding. Audsley. Dodd, Mead & Co. New York. (1905).

Lecture Notes - Cyril Ward. Leigh Historical Society. (1960).

Matter Relating To the Organ. Pendlebury, Leigh. (1928).

The Modern British Organ. A. Weekes & Co. London. Noel A. Bonavia-Hunt M.A.